SELF-POLLUTION

A Thinking Journey to Clear Fear and Anger

DR. TAHA "PACEMAKER"

BALBOA
PRESS
A DIVISION OF HAY HOUSE

Balboa Press books may be ordered through booksellers or by contacting:

Balboa Press
A Division of Hay House
1663 Liberty Drive
Bloomington, IN 47403
www.balboapress.com
1 (877) 407-4847

Because of the dynamic nature of the Internet, any web addresses or
links contained in this book may have changed since publication and
may no longer be valid. The views expressed in this work are solely those
of the author and do not necessarily reflect the views of the publisher,
and the publisher hereby disclaims any responsibility for them.

The author of this book does not dispense medical advice or prescribe the use
of any technique as a form of treatment for physical, emotional, or medical
problems without the advice of a physician, either directly or indirectly. The
intent of the author is only to offer information of a general nature to help
you in your quest for emotional and spiritual well-being. In the event you use
any of the information in this book for yourself, which is your constitutional
right, the author and the publisher assume no responsibility for your actions.

Any people depicted in stock imagery provided by Thinkstock are models,
and such images are being used for illustrative purposes only.
Certain stock imagery © Thinkstock.

Printed in the United States of America.

ISBN: 978-1-4525-9863-5 (sc)
ISBN: 978-1-4525-9864-2 (hc)
ISBN: 978-1-4525-9862-8 (e)

Library of Congress Control Number: 2014920038

Balboa Press rev. date: 12/1/2014

THANK YOU

Thank you for the life … and for being in your life.

I was born with nothing … You made me something.

My hands were empty … You filled them with your heart.

You created the universe for me … and it will end with me.

Thank you for every breath … I loved the beauty of your earth.

You thought me everything … You let me think, feel, and see.

Thank you for the mountains and rivers …
hills, sky, trees, and flowers.

The moon breaks my night … The sun
shines and falls beyond my sight.

Thank you for the soul … It was a dress,
torn … I couldn't repair it all.

I talked, walked, fell, and rose … learned, read, and wrote.

Many people I met … I wasn't aware
they were there for me to test.

I laughed, cried, hated, and fought …
repeated my mistakes and thoughts.

Thank you for the bread … Billions of people are fed.

My eyes were blind, my heart was unkind …
my hands made my life lines.

It was a journey of birds flew … I will miss them all, when I go.

I miss to kiss many caring hands … They
filled my soul with everything kind.

Tomorrow, there will be no noise … but the
echo of love will make a lasting voice.

CONTENTS

INTRODUCTION

This book presents my personal concepts on human thinking. It is a journey of the "self," from the cavepeople who built civilizations to those who reached the moon yet still remained vulnerable because of a greedy and insecure ego.

Human thinking, beliefs, and emotions are dominated by the ego. Without the ego, humans would live without interest in competing, comparing, or progressing. The ego makes humans the most inelegant and emotional beasts—an "ego-minded herd."

Human behavior is stimulating and reflective. Children are programmed from an early age by their parents, their culture, and the media, all of which pollute genetic behavior and manufacture human beings with acquired personal specifications.

Human emotions are cumulative, chronic, and dormant. In fear, humans not only run away or fight (fight or flight); they may faint or develop chronic fears, phobias, shyness, stress, anger, and mental-health conditions.

Self-Pollution is a continuation of my previous book, *Self-Conditioning and Sexuality*. It is based on my personal concepts of the *mind pacemaker*, the source of subconscious thoughts, mind beats, dreams, and mental illnesses.

The book also offers explanations and therapeutic techniques for many negative thoughts and emotions, including fear and anger, and explores new concepts of thinking on instincts, sanity elements, sexuality, sexual orientation, child abuse, and the "E-spot."

CHAPTER 1

SELF-CONDITIONING

The "self" starts with a single fertilized cell, which divides into a human being. The genes of the cell determine the physical looks and the instinctive behaviors of the newborn at birth but do not fill the memory. The environment fills a person's empty memory and determines his or her mental growth within the womb or within a culture.

During pregnancy, hormones, chemicals, and certain foods or drugs can affect the growth of embryos' organs. After birth, family, culture, and the media program humans' inherited instincts. Parents may have the choice to have children, but children have no choice but to accept their environmental conditioning.

Conditioning is a "programming" process of the adaptation of the internal environment (inherited genetic instincts) to the surrounding environment (e.g., family and culture). An infant's environment is dominated by his or her caregivers, who have a major role in his or her conditioning. Parents program their children's minds with certain skills, languages, roles, values, traditions, beliefs, and acceptable and unacceptable behaviors.

Children born in India or China, for example, acquire Indian or Chinese behaviors, acceptable to their respective environments. They are culturally conditioned in the first few years of life.

Traveling around the world, we meet people who behave, react, speak, and dress according to their cultural traditions. Just like environmental pollution, cultural conditioning can "pollute" inherited behavior or change "pure self" to a "conditioned self" and can irreversibly delete the human superego or humanity. Wars give people a license to kill both innocent and abusive people without trial or mercy.

The impact of environment on human genes can be recognized by watching twins who carry identical sets of genes and share physical looks but are separated after birth. Their behavior changes if they are brought up by different parents who have different religions and live in different countries.

Unlike other animals, humans are born with an expanding ego. The ego is the selfish energy within each human. It charges people to act or have everything the self desires without sharing or considering others. The ego can drive the human to become an inventor or an abuser, a creator or a destroyer. It inspires infants to walk, talk, and learn like their parents, siblings, or peers, while children raised in orphanages, if they are neglected and receive no care, may behave like mentally disabled people. Without exposure to life's temptations, inspiration, support, or education, the egos of such neglected children will shrink, and they will live a primitive life.

The environment can inspire the human ego to build dreams and destinies. In certain environments, children are inspired by their families, cultures, or media to be rich or become professionals—teachers, lawyers, engineers, artists, or singers. Children's dreams become subconscious "ego desires," creating a mental energy that drives them to achieve their ambitions, but the ego's greed, pride, and abusiveness have delayed human progress for millions of years. It took human beings many centuries to invent digital technology.

The human ego has an unlimited ability to expand in positive (creative) or negative (destructive) directions. It is programmed in childhood by family, culture, and the media to generate ego desires, or an "ego enemy." The latter includes anyone who threatens or interferes with achieving the self-desires. On a daily basis, people make ego desires and ego enemies at home, work, or in public places.

Childhood experiences are saved in the memory for years and can determine the person's ego behavior, pride, and greed. Support, care, and motivation can inspire children to grow into independent, creative, productive, caring professionals while neglect, abuse, or lack of care and moral discipline can make children emotionally dependent, greedy, vulnerable, or unable to achieve their ego desires without the abuse of self or others.

Religions evolved to inhibit the expansion and greed of the human ego. However, ego desires remain more powerful than religion, and many religions are based on ego desires for "heaven" for the *self* and "hell" for the ego enemy. This can make the human ego vulnerable to abuse, as the person is willing to accept it in order to enter heaven. Throughout history, people and leaders have repeated their religious killings and wars, as their "holy" ego desire is inherited from their parents.

Fear plays a major role in human behavior. However, the human ego only fears death. Its greed for life can make people lie, cheat, deceive, and perform any immoral or abusive behavior secretly to avoid legal punishment, stigmas, taboos, or hell. People and nations can evade the fear of national or international law and punishment by making allies to support their abuse.

Anything that prevents people from achieving an ego desire represents a threat to the ego. A perceived ego threat provokes the negative emotions of stress, fear, hate, or anger. These emotions generate harmful negative energy, impair rational thinking, and drive people to abuse themselves and others and pollute this planet.

The ego has prevented partners, parents, siblings, friends, groups, and nations from trusting each other or uniting. It drives people to build overly secure houses, "cages," national borders, and nuclear bombs to deter the ego enemy.

The insecure human ego also drives people to be followers of their cultural norms in order to avoid being considered unsociable, unacceptable, odd, or alien. For example, the behavior of Indians or Africans may be regarded as unacceptable in European cultures. Similarly, fanatical people would not accept any behavior against their own.

History books are "ego books" filled with ego pride and ego enemies. They are written differently according to each country's viewpoint. People relate to their pasts, childhoods, or history books, and many live in the past's pride or pain and cannot move into the future. They may follow their beliefs or religion, but when they face threats to their ego desires, they tend to ignore their spiritual beliefs.

Cultural conditioning has changed human behavior into an acquired one. It has polluted people's instinctive behaviors and emotions to the extent that they have difficulty describing the inherited *self* with which they were born. There is no diagnostic test that can differentiate an inherited self from an acquired one. Meditation can bring people inside their inner selves (or souls) for a few minutes or hours, but thereafter, they wake up to face reality.

People are programmed, hypnotized, to follow cultural traditions, values, rituals, habits, routines, laws, policies, media, social classes, economies, beliefs, resources, and certain sexualities as a norm. Childhood programming can drive a few people to be heroes and a few to be serial killers. Mind programming cannot be deleted easily after the childhood period, but we may clear "self-pollution," the negative energy of fear, hate, and anger, from our mind "pacemaker."

The universe's pacemaker is clicking, making an irreversible time journey, but the human mind's pacemaker relates to the past. Time steals our youth, the past, and the future but not our emotions. People keep their love or hate even after death. They may never forgive their dead abusive parent, sibling, peer, or leader.

The "power of the now," or silent pause in time, can't bring lasting peace, but the "power of behavior" can. The behavior of animals, humans, angels and evils are different. They can generate positive or negative emotions and a lasting love or hate memory and history. Every second that passes is a drop in the ocean of the past, expanding the universe and human history beyond the mind limitations.

CHAPTER 2

BASIC INSTINCTS
(INHERITED BEHAVIOR)

Regardless of cultural conditioning, people share many instincts with other mammals. Basic instincts are unlearned, inherited behaviors that save the species from extinction. Instinctive behavior is automatic and irresistible; it has enabled mammals to reproduce for millions of years. Although humans are one of the most intelligent animals, infants would not survive or develop intelligence without nursing, training, and education. In contrast, many animals and insects are born with inherited skillful behaviors (e.g., birds swimming and migrating or the collaborative work of bees and ants).

Unlearned human behavior is the inherited personality traits, which can be recognized in the first few weeks after birth. Each newborn shows different moods, body movements, sleep patterns, and reactions to internal and external sensory stimuli. Infants also have different voices, smiles, and interactions with other people or objects. The inherited behaviors of humans and animals (e.g., domestic pets) may gradually be changed into learned behavior by their caregivers. Humans share many basic instincts with other mammals, such as:

1. caring, feeding, and protecting (superego) (e.g., female to newborn)
2. dominating (ego) (e.g., male toward individual or group)
3. trusting (belief system) in the surrounding environment
4. thinking, learning, understanding, and remembering (advanced in humans)
5. emotions (e.g., being easily startled from acute fear or anger at abuse)
6. feelings (e.g., pain from injury or comfort from offering care)
7. belonging to the same species (e.g., animal herd)
8. bonding (e.g., parents to newborn)
9. searching for place, food, comfort, or company
10. compulsion for food at hunger, drink at thirst
11. disgust at certain smells, such as feces or certain gases
12. hostility or aggression (more in males and nursing females)
13. rejection, desertion (e.g., abandonment of the newborn)
14. play (e.g., cubs with their mother or siblings)
15. submission (e.g., to group commands in the herd)
16. neurological reflexes (e.g. sneezing, yawning, limb jerking, coughing)
17. consciousness reflexes: sleep, wakefulness, alertness
18. tiredness and weakness after exertion or illness
19. producing sounds (e.g., at excitement, panic, or anger)
20. sex (desire, impulse and reproduction)

Sanity is the behavior that differentiates the sane from the insane person or animal. Human sanity, however, is subjective behavior within cultural norms. People who live in the jungle may practice certain rituals, such as drinking blood or urine, which may be considered insane for urban people.

Although infants are born with similar instincts, each culture produces different human models with different behaviors and languages. People raised in Asia, Europe, Africa, India, China, or America are conditioned to their particular cultural values, traditions, habits, vocal tones, accents, expressions, and body language. Environment can also affect the physical looks over millions of years.

In addition to basic instincts, the five senses are the receptors for human external feelings. Without senses, there would be no self-identity, feeling, or environment, and humans would not survive danger. The presence of the five senses can subject humans to physical and mental comfort or pain and can expand the human ego and emotions to extreme limits. Vision is a safety tool. It can protect us from danger, but addiction to Internet games, gambling, or porn can waste hours of productivity and creativity.

During sleep, people lose their senses, feeling, identities, and history and become vulnerable and open to danger. They cannot sleep in the wild without protection. In the city, they build houses to protect themselves from their greedy, insecure, distrustful ego enemies. Sleeping adults may share similar behavioral patterns with sleeping infants or animals, but after sleep, they regain their egos, personal identities, memories, histories, habits, moods, pride, shame, love, hate, anger, fear, and greed.

CHAPTER 3

SANITY ELEMENTS

The advanced learning and understanding capacity in humans is empowered by a long-term memory store that can retain events from early childhood until death and transform acute emotions into chronic positive or negative behaviors.

Sanity and intelligence are subjective within each culture. Corrupt leaders or politicians may be regarded as very intelligent in certain cultures, while people donating their fortunes to animal charities may be considered insane. In the jungle, a sane human follows the tribe's rituals, which may include cannibalism. Both jungle and urban dwellers are followers of their cultural traditions; if they are not, they may be regarded as abnormal, different, eccentric, or insane. Even geniuses or professors may be regarded as insane if their behavior does not match the cultural norm.

Humans have an unlimited learning capacity. The psychology of human behavior evolves with the development of human culture. With more civil rights in the developed countries, certain previously unacceptable behavior becomes acceptable and vice versa. Spectra of autistic and attention deficient disorders have become more recognized than they were before. Homosexuality was considered a mental illness before the 1970s in psychology textbooks; it has become a normal behavior in certain cultures. In contrast, pedophilia, which was a common behavior in many cultures, committed by abusers who were proud to shame and stigmatize vulnerable children, has become a criminal act.

Other types of abuse are committed daily by "normal" people. According to cultural norms, they are regarded as sane. Physically or emotionally abusive behavior of a father, brother, relative, neighbor, peer, colleague, manager, leader, or politician can trigger stress, anxiety, fear, hate, anger, depression, mental illnesses, and psychosomatic diseases in other people but is still considered normal behavior in many cultures.

Human sanity has different levels. Its highest level represents the mental ability to survive and progress in life without negative thoughts, emotions, feelings, abuse, and psychosomatic or mental illnesses. Many genetic illnesses are triggered by environmental factors, such as stress, including asthma, migraines, IBS, diabetes, heart disease, high blood pressure, and certain cancers and skin diseases. However, sane people cannot stop environmental pollution or stress, as their mentality is influenced by the ten main inherited instincts listed here. The genetic thresholds and the environmental programming "pollution" of these instincts influence the level of human sanity. These ten instincts mirror human sanity elements and include:

1. thinking
2. memory
3. ego
4. superego
5. belief
6. emotions
7. feeling
8. learning
9. understanding
10. behavior

Genetically, each person is born with different thresholds for each instinct. This may mean that people born with high ego and low superego thresholds tend to be ruthless or abusers, while people born with low ego and high superego thresholds tend to be caring, supportive, or peaceful. However, the childhood environment (parents, culture, or media) has a major impact on modifying human sanity elements and crafting people's personalities, behaviors, and sexualities.

Thinking, learning, understanding, and remembering are more advanced in humans than other mammals and help them to build civilizations. However, it took millions of years for humans to reach the moon. The delay of humans' scientific progress is largely related to their insecure egos. The human ego can't survive without "ego breaks" of rest, pleasure, greed, or abuse, and human sanity is predominately influenced by the ego judgment. The ego can undermine all other sanity elements and dominate human thinking. Additionally, the five senses, particularly vision, are the most powerful tools for the human ego's desire and abuse. Without vision, there would be no civilization, technology, art, media, transport, shopping, makeup, fashion, photography, pornography, seduction, hunting, or abuse.

My concept of thinking is based on the *thinking pacemaker*, which is similar to a heart's pacemaker but is attached to the memory store in the brain and generates nonstop *thought beats*, or "mind beats." This pacemaker represents the subconscious mind, or the involuntary inner brain noises, which generates nonstop thoughts twenty-four/seven. During sleep, the mind pacemaker decelerates and generates dreams. Before bedtime, if the mind pacemaker's beats were accelerated (e.g., through stress, anger, or fear), it would lead to obsession, insomnia, or nightmares.

The mind pacemaker has a daily rhythm. It slows during sleep and recharges in the morning with thoughts. Newborns have long sleep periods, as their mind pacemakers are nearly empty of thoughts. Abnormality of the mind pacemaker (or "arrhythmia" of mind beats), such as uncontrolled obsessive thinking, can lead to insomnia, nightmares, psychosomatic diseases, mental illnesses, psychoses, or schizophrenia, while its degeneration can lead to confusion or dementia.

Conditioning, or programming of the mind pacemaker (particularly the ego during early childhood), has a major impact on our subconscious behavior and judgment (belief system), which gradually becomes biased by our ego desires. Even in court, unless there is clear evidence, criminals, victims, judges, barristers, and lawyers may use their ego judgments to win money, pride, or fame with their cases.

The strong ego desire for money, fame, titles, or revenge against ego enemies can impair human moral beliefs and rational thinking. It can drive politicians, leaders, judges, or barristers to use different angles of the law to gain their ego desires. Most ego desires can be achieved with money, which has made urbanized people "money-minded," selfish, greedy, and distrustful, leading them to end their close personal and social relationships or sell their possessions or their bodies for money.

People do not trust strangers with their money or children. However, their egos would accept strangers if they spoiled them with money, rewards, power, positions, titles, or fame. Politicians often deal with dictators, criminals, or terrorists in order to achieve their ego desires or to destroy their ego enemies. The ego also drives nations to make racist political and discriminatory religious propaganda.

The ego power can delete willpower, or self-trust. People's strong desire for another person makes them "fall in love." Their ego desire shrinks their willpower, preventing them from making rational or impartial judgments. After marriage, the ego desire may fade away and that desirable person may limit the person's personal goals and freedom or become a distrusted, selfish ego enemy.

Similarly, the strong ego desire for sex makes people hide their STDs or HIV-positive status and weakens their willpower so they have casual sex without using protection. Every year, millions of men and women transmit HIV, and many infants acquire HIV in utero from their mothers.

The ego has made people more harmful to themselves and to one another than most vicious animals. Beasts from the same species living in groups or herds may unite to kill prey, but rarely do they kill members of their own species. Throughout history, humans have had endless wars or desires to abuse or kill their ego enemies.

The conditioning or programming of the mind pacemaker has major impacts on human behavior. The mind pacemaker is linked to memory and the autonomic nervous system (ANS). The latter is an "emotions store." During thinking, we identify with past thoughts saved in the memory store, and these thoughts are judged by the ego in a spectrum range from ego desire to ego enemy. The *programmed ego* makes its judgment within a second and stimulates the ANS to secrete hormones and neurotransmitters (H/N) that make us feel happy, comfortable, manic, sad, stressed, worried, fearful, panicked, angry, or nothing at all.

Creation & invention Positive feeling Ego desire for progress		
Ego threat → tendency to abuse self with negative emotions such as feeling guilty, shy, worried, stress, anxiety, panic, phobic, embarrassed, fear of losing (money, job, pride, person, position, reputation), obsession, rumination, jealousy, envy, hate, anger, hostility, abuse or avoidance behaviour, insomnia, nightmares, hopelessness, depression, isolation, suicide	**Ego** **&** **TEBE** **pacemaker**	**Ego power** → tendency to abuse others: reject, ignore, disrespect, neglect, bulling, undermining, marginalizing, discriminating, separation, isolation, insulting, threatening, assaulting, abuse (emotional abuse, financial abuse, physical abuse, institutional abuse, sexual abuse, rape, media abuse or racism), hate, aggression, anger, counter hate (hostility, revenge, abuse, wars)
Ego desire for pleasure Obsession & addiction		

Diagram-1: shows human "Thinking – Ego –Belief - Emotions" pacemaker, which is dominated by the ego.

Diagram 1 shows the link between *thinking, ego, belief,* and *emotions.* They form the TEBE, or mind pacemaker, which is linked to memory and the ANS. During early childhood, the TEBE is "programmed" according to family and cultural values and generates our programmed subconscious mind beats. Every thought crossing the mind or generated by the mind pacemaker is judged by the ego first. The ego acts as a personal belief system by which the person judges life events according to the ego desire-enemy spectrum. Ego judgment triggers the ANS to release H/N, or emotions, accordingly. Strong emotions release H/N, which affix childhood events with emotions in the memory as dormant emotional thoughts, like software files, for decades. These emotional memories become references for our subconscious mind during adulthood.

For example, a father abuses his son. The son's ego judges his father as an ego enemy. The abuse triggers the ANS to release H/N during displays of fear, anger, or sex. The H/N saves the events of abuse in the TEBE memory store as thoughts with negative emotions. If the father remains abusive toward the son, he becomes an ego threat to the son's ego desire. Repeated thinking about the abuser and his actions generates negative anger emotions, which impair the child's rational thinking, behavior, and performance at home or at school (left box). The child may escape the ego threat by secretly practicing his ego desire or pleasure (bottom box). If the child grows up and gains physical or financial power, he may abuse or neglect his abuser (right box).

In contrast, a supportive and caring father might inspire his son's ego to be creative, inventive, or professional (top box). Gradually, the saved thoughts and emotions in the TEBE pacemaker program the subconscious mind, just like programming a computer with software. These "files" become references for future ego judgment. TEBE programming cannot be easily deleted from the memory, unless the child changes his environment and receives proper long-term care and support.

Human emotions are cumulative and are saved as chronic emotional thoughts in their memories. Children's stored thoughts influence their adult subconscious behavior. Fear and anger are influenced by the programming of the ego in early childhood. If children have no power to resolve the threat (left box), they suffer chronic negative emotions for years (e.g., shyness, stress, anxiety, hate, etc.). These emotions can impair their rational thinking, confidence, and performance or may drive children to lie, cheat, or fake emotions in order to escape pain, punishment, and abuse by their ego enemy. Chronic negative emotions can also drive children to commit antisocial acts, escape to the ego-desirable behaviors, fantasize, or engage in secretive behaviors of pleasure (bottom box).

The human ego can't live without curiosity, pride, vanity, judgment, pleasure, greed, abuse, or counterabuse. Human behavior is reflective, stimulating, or contagious. Children and adults are curious and try to copy any behavior that brings self-pleasure. However, any pleasurable behavior is liable to addiction. Many urbanites have acquired different types of addictions to pleasurable habits, such as smoking, drinking alcohol, overeating, shopping, TV watching, Internet surfing, gambling, illicit drug use, pornography, and masturbation. Without moral support or inhibition, the ego is curious and can desire everything that brings pleasure or comfort to the self.

Most human ego desires are achieved through money, which can buy pleasure or power (physical, managerial, military, or nuclear). Urbanites are programmed to become money-minded to achieve ego desires, while cavepeople had no need to have a bank account, bank loans, or mortgages. Ego expansion and greed increase with the increase of temptations in the city. In contrast, cavepeople faced limited temptations and had limited ego greed, addictions, and mental illnesses. They didn't fear poverty or losing their bank credit and did not suffer from shopping or Internet addictions, OCD, anorexia, bulimia, or other eating disorders.

In both civilized and corrupt cultures, parents are the first to praise or blame. Unlike in other mammals, human parents have the choice and the desire to make children. Their children have no choice but to accept them. Parents can support and inspire their children to be creators, inventors, or healers, but they also generate abusers or criminals. Parents are the first child abusers if they are incapable of looking after the moral, emotional, educational, and financial welfare of their children until they reach an independent age. Selfish parents marry to have children and then get divorced to fulfill their ego desires. Their children suffer alone and may become abusers, victims of abuse, or both.

Political leaders are also child abusers if they ignore supporting abused children or providing child support measures in their country. Thousands of criminals enter prison on a daily basis all over the world, but many abusers, corrupt politicians, leaders, dictators, and terrorists evade prison and continue to abuse others.

They were born innocent to neglectful, incompetent, selfish, or irresponsible parents. The law blames and punishes the criminals and ignores the selfish, incompetent, irresponsible parents and the system that generated criminals and abusers.

Following are discussions of the sanity elements.

Thinking

Thinking is the beginning and the end of the human story. Humans are "thinking beings," created with the ability to think, imagine, and fantasize. Thinking has created human tribes, cultures, nations, religions, politics, science, technology, art, literature, and history. Thinking is the main source of people's judgments, beliefs, decisions, desires, intellect, planning, progress, successes, failures, moods, emotions, obsessions, memories, conflicts, addictions, abuses, wars, and mental illnesses.

We cannot stop thinking, as we have a thinking "mind pacemaker," which generates involuntary, nonstop thoughts, or mind beats, continuously, twenty-four-seven. These beats represent the human subconscious mind. They slow down during sleep and produce our unconscious dreams. The mind pacemaker links the human's *thinking*, *ego*, *belief*, and *emotions*, forming a TEBE pacemaker, which is often dominated by the ego's judgment, desires, and threats.

Genetically, each person has a unique thinking pacemaker (it is like fingerprints), which represents personal mental activity and self-identity. It is not duplicated, even in identical twins. The diversity of human thinking has helped people invent, create, write, read, design, and build technology and civilizations.

The quality of human thinking has been divided into genius, intelligent, talented, average, below average, or learning disabled. However, most human thoughts are acquired after birth and education can improve inherited thinking thresholds. Children are born without thoughts. Their empty minds acquire thoughts from their families, cultures, or media, which program their minds and behaviors. Without education, humans might live a primitive life. Fanatical education may also create a primitive culture full of followers of "holy" thoughts, including inequality, discrimination, hate, abuse, or killing.

Most thinking is influenced by programming of the mind TEBE pacemaker in early childhood. Childhood thoughts are saved as dormant emotional thoughts in the memory store, which is linked to the TEBE pacemaker and to the ANS. The saved emotional thoughts in the memory become reference "software" for the future thinking processes of the subconscious mind. In adulthood, people relate life events they come across to their saved emotional thoughts. Thinking activates, relates, or retrieves their programmed past emotional thoughts, triggering the ANS to generate different levels of emotions and feelings that influence their behavior.

To simplify, I divided thinking into active and passive thinking. Each type subdivides into negative and positive thinking. Active thinking occurs when we use our mind pacemaker to generate our own thoughts during writing, communicating, criticizing, searching, planning, imagining, remembering, fantasizing, interpreting, analyzing, filtering, anticipating, judging, answering questions, or solving problems or puzzles. Active thinking can be triggered by need, curiosity, crisis, serendipity, inspiration, ego desire, abuse, or sensory stimuli, such as touching, hearing, smelling, driving, watching TV, or listening to a conversation or to music. In a certain place, active thoughts may suddenly develop and evolve into a notion, song, poem, story, or discovery or may inspire people to change their lifestyles, beliefs, religions, partners, careers, cities, or countries.

Inventing, discovering, and creative thinking and writing are active thinking abilities that can be acquired through education and training and have helped people build technology and civilizations, as well as military weapons to destroy ego-enemy civilizations. Active thinking may trigger passive thinking. For example, while preparing for an exam, involuntary passive thoughts or dormant emotional thoughts can subconsciously interfere with our reading.

Passive thinking represents our subconscious mind's thoughts generated by our mind TEBE pacemaker as brain "noise," especially when we are alone or are not communicating with others. Most human thinking is passive and represents recycling of past thoughts saved in our memory store as emotional thoughts. As shown in diagram 1, thinking is dominated by ego desire and ego threat. The ego is influenced by the cultural conditioning and programming of the TEBE pacemaker during early childhood. The programming of the mind pacemaker during childhood modifies people's inherited instinctive thinking thresholds, reactions, and behaviors.

Active and passive thinking triggers different levels of emotions. We laugh when we remember funny events and are upset when we think about abuse. We feel hungry when we think about food and sexually aroused when we think of sex. In contrast, emotions may trigger thinking. When hungry, we think of getting food, and when we fall in love, we think of marriage or having a family. Thinking may be impaired by physical, medical, and mental illness (e.g., depression), strong emotions, sexual desire, drugs, alcohol, sleep, anesthesia, and dementia.

Imagining and fantasizing are active thinking and helped humans create, design, and build colorful cities, buildings, technology, arts, fashion, furniture, monuments, toys, and gifts. Fantasy is an escape from the reality or daily routine to the world of ego. Human ego can't survive without self-pleasure, including abusive acts. It tends to escape boring reality by practicing pleasurable behavior, such as smoking, eating, watching TV, or surfing the Internet. Any pleasurable thoughts can lead to obsession, addiction, and compulsion, and many people become obsessed with one or more ego desires.

Conditioning in early life programs human thinking, or the TEBE pacemaker, with "cultural software" and provides children with a mother language, body language, emotional reactions, and eating and drinking habits common to their cultures. Parents fill their children's empty memory stores with cultural behaviors, roles, and values. Children save life events as emotional thoughts. Strong emotions trigger the ANS to secrete hormones and neurotransmitters (H/N), which save childhood emotional events in the memory store for decades.

The programming of children's TEBE is influenced by their ego. It becomes their personal belief system by which they judge life events according to their ego desirable-enemy spectrum (e.g., ego desirable, ego undesirable, ego safe, ego unsafe, ego enemy, or ego threat). For example, children's egos judge their caregivers as ego desirable or safe when their caregiver gives them food and comfort.

Genetically, some people are born as fast thinkers; others may develop their thoughts and ideas over days or never. Deep thinkers tend to be creative, confident, independent leaders while poor thinkers tend to be superficial, insecure, dependent followers. Both can be idealistic or pragmatic, caring or ruthless, and many fail to read the thoughts of others. A few children may inherit a high IQ or superior ability to think, analyze, or solve difficult questions or puzzles. However, without the opportunity for education, their talent may fail to develop. Education can also improve the thinking abilities of people with average IQs, while fanatical beliefs can keep their minds fixated on past thoughts.

Obsession is a type of repeated thinking usually associated with ego desire and threat. People tend to be obsessed with ego desires (e.g., money, power, fame, food, pleasure, or sex). They also develop obsessions if their ego desire is under threat or their ego pride is injured. The injured ego may suffer pain from shame and search for support or for pleasurable thoughts and behaviors. Certain inherited personality traits are vulnerable to obsession with certain thoughts, particularly when the person is alone, bored, or stressed. Obsessions can impair objective thinking, limit people's productivity, and evolve into certain compulsive behaviors, like practicing the same rituals every day (such as washing one's hands many times a day).

Thinking can be influenced by age, sex, time, experience, cultural values, beliefs, religion, and education. Younger generations are conditioned to express their thoughts, desires, and goals differently than elderly people. Men and women may think differently. Women may cry watching a romantic movie, while men may get bored watching the same movie. People from certain cultures may be inspired by a specific holy book, while other cultures may reject the same book. Every nation has a certain type of political thinking—often using propaganda to brainwash people with subjective thinking. Fanatical people tend to have a fixed belief system, or one way of thinking, which includes rejecting thoughts that go against their "holy" thoughts.

Despite people's different-thinking pacemakers, they may share similar cultural thoughts or judgments regarding certain behaviors, such as women behaving in a masculine way or men behaving in a feminine way. We may also laugh and cry watching certain behaviors or movies. Science and education can expand humans' thinking capacity, perception, productivity, creativity, and contributions to new interventions. In contrast, accumulated academic experience may lead to more doubt, fear, stress, and confusion. Many mental illnesses are related to the way we think of our ego pride, which has been threatened, injured, or damaged.

The attacked ego can subject the mind pacemaker to the acceleration of mind beats or obsession. Fear or anger may cause obsession with the same negative emotional thoughts, stress, insomnia, nightmares, or depression. In contrast, positive thinking can be used to treat mental illnesses by allowing us to skip the ego and the past thoughts or change the way we think of our ego enemies. Electrocardioversion has been used to reverse irregular heartbeats or arrhythmias, while electrical shocks to the brain, or EEG, have been used to reverse irregular mind beats in people with acute psychosis.

Memory

Memory is storage for the events we have saved in the mind during our life journey. Just like the heart pacemaker is linked to the heart chambers, the memory is linked to the mind's TEBE pacemaker and the ANS or the emotional store. The memory store saves past events, learned experiences, and skills that can help humans survive on a daily basis. Dementia erases the knowledge that protects people from danger. A demented person may leave food burning on the stove or get lost, unable to remember his or her address.

People have a unique long-term memory, which can expand by learning and education from childhood until death, but events linked to strong emotions (e.g., success, abuse, fearful, and erotic) are mainly saved in the memory and may influence their behavior, relationships, social interactions, careers, physical and mental health, and sexuality. At birth, newborns have empty memories; they are a blank page. They may behave like a demented person who has no experience with which to look after him- or herself and may die without nursing or feeding. Their parents start to program their memories with their personal and cultural "software."

However, each child is born with different inherited interests and receives and saves the surrounding events and conditions differently. Siblings are born with curious egos, which drive them to ask questions and learn skills that attract their egos' attention. The competency of the five senses is important in receiving and storing life events. Without the five senses, children would not receive external sensory sensations and would not acquire memory or feeling.

Human ego determination is more powerful than disability. Many talented deaf and blind people have proven that eyes and ears are unnecessary for them to compete with their peers. Blind people have used touch to gain an advantage that many sighted people could not achieve. This may also reflect that vision can interfere with people's education and storing of knowledge. Sighted people usually store events as emotional images or videos. During thinking, they relate to their past visual experiences, which were saved in their memories as emotional images. They are programmed to make a visual judgment on people within seconds, while a blind person would not be affected by others' physical appearance.

Humans are born with different memory strengths. A powerful memory can correlate with intelligence. People with high IQs tend to save memories for decades. A powerful memory could be a source of happiness or misery. Painful or fearful memories of abuse during childhood may last for many decades and may cause the TEBE pacemaker or subconscious thinking to malfunction and induce chronic negative emotions that can trigger many symptoms (such as avoidance behavior, phobias, panic attacks, insomnia, nightmares, personality disorders, sexuality disorders, poor communication skills, poor self-esteem or confidence, and depression). The saved ego desires and threats in the memory are the main sources of human conflicts, counterabuse, hate, anger, separation, divorce, infidelity, promiscuity, prostitution, homicide, suicide, terrorism, and wars.

Memory represents self-identity. Each person tends to store a specific type of memory. The differences are influenced by people's ages, genders, sanity elements, interests, family, and cultural and media values. Time and age may fade away many emotional thoughts from our memories. There is also a difference in the way men and women store their memories. Ask an old married couple about their wedding events, and each one will tell a different story despite their being together during the event.

Abuse and sexual histories are among the most powerful memories. This may be because of the following:

- These memories are associated with strong emotions of fear, anger, or excitement, which trigger the release of hormones and neurotransmitters (H/N) that help to fix the events in the memory.

- Humans tend to save strong emotional events that stimulate their inherited interests and relate to their past experience. Watching, hearing, or reading similar events can cause retrieval of the old emotional memory.

- Repetition of thinking on the same events increase their fixation in the memory, just like repeating a song many times a day would.

- Ego desire makes people repeat similar behavior. People interested in football tend to remember football players better than their phone number.

Memory can be temporarily impaired by drugs, alcohol, and illness, but without dementia being a root cause, it cannot be easily erased.

Anger is the most harmful emotional memory for the self and others. It is the main cause of daily conflicts, domestic abuse, divorce, dismissal, depression, insomnia, homicides, massacres, wars, and many mental-health and psychosomatic illnesses. Anger is usually caused by the inability of people to accept ego threats, abuse, damage, injury, failure, loss, or death or the inability to forgive the people who abuse the ego. Anger generates negative energy, which can paralyze the mind, preventing it from thinking rationally or wisely, and leaves the subconscious mind with a vicious cycle of hate and revenge. This negative memory can blind the subconscious and keep it from accepting self-mistakes or the truth behind the abusive events. Anger links people even after death, and some refuse to accept any positive contribution from their abusers or their ego enemies for decades or ever.

Deleting angry memories can be difficult in people with high ego pride, who are unable to forgive their ego enemies or who reject understanding of human nature or the truth. Angry people cannot accept their limitations and mistakes in dealing with the distrustful human ego. They also cannot accept the negative impact of their behavior on their ego enemies and the limitations of their ego enemies. They have a strong belief or affirmation that their behavior is right and their ego enemies' behavior is unforgivable.

Medical or psychological therapy may help to improve people's anger; changing environment, career, or country may too, but changes start from within and people need to change their way of thinking and build up new, happy memories, hobbies, or relationships. They need to accept human distrustful egos and avoid taking risks, repeating similar mistakes, and watching daily racist news, propaganda, or drama. Painful memories of domestic violence, divorce, abuse, suicides, homicides, terrorism, international conflicts, and wars cannot be stopped by sedatives or drugs.

Lack of memory (due to dementia, for example) can make people lose their happy memories, talents, skills, and creativity. They may become dependent and unable to remember names, times, dates, places, events, or simple safety skills. A demented man may urinate in his bed and forget where he needs to go to relieve himself.

Ego

The ego is a self-desire energy, which drives the human to act or have everything, without sharing or considering responsibility toward others. The human ego has unlimited desire for life's temptations, which may only end in the grave. The ego energy charges humans to be curious, inquisitive, pleasure-seeking, greedy, insecure, paranoid, disloyal, possessive, mean, proud, arrogant, ungrateful, selfish, rude, bored, stubborn, vain, unfaithful, dominating, dismissive, obstructive, destructive, judgmental, biased, secretive, deceitful, prone to cheating, dishonest, distrustful, envious, jealous, impulsive, vengeful, bullying, vulgar, insulting, hostile, abusive, or counterabusive.

The human ego can also charge people with a strong, persistent attraction, interest, imagination, fantasy, and determination. It gives the energy to build personal desires, goals, careers, inventions, fame, titles, power, fortunes, homes, cities, and civilizations.

However, it can't work continuously, twenty-four/seven, without an "ego break," e.g., rest, pleasure, greed, or abuse. Ego breaks may take hours or even years. Many people become addicted to pleasure and fail to achieve their ego desires. Threats or failure to achieve ego desires is the main cause of abuse of the self and others. Ego failure can cause anger, which can paralyze impartial thinking and keep people's minds obsessed with negative energy. Ego greed for money, power, authority, titles, pride, fame, vanity, or sex has made people insecure, distrustful, and abusive to themselves and others.

DIAGRAM 2: TAHA'S CARICATURE OF THE EGO

There is no "id," as human instincts are programmed (polluted) and lose their purity after birth. Children have empty memories at birth, which are filled gradually by learning. Their acquired learning experience conditions their instincts after birth according to the surrounding environment, and their programmed egos start to judge their acquired thoughts, feelings, beliefs, and behaviors.

The human ego has endless self-greed, which makes people love life and fear death or wish death on their enemies. Every day, the ego generates an "ego desire" and "ego enemy" subconsciously when people meet others or watch sports, news, or religious programs. The ego is insecure and liable to become obsessed with its desires and threats. Obsessing over the threats that interfere with achieving ego desires can make people unable to think "outside the box" or think wisely. It can drive them to be highly negative, withdrawn, panicked, angry, or abusive to themselves or others.

The ego has endless lists of desires for possession or greed, and the list may end in the grave. Luckily, the earth was created to feed millions of people for millions of years. The ego also has abusive energy, and people have endless lists of hated or undesirable objects. Their lists may end in separation, fights, court cases, or wars. Even after abusing its enemies, the ego keeps generating more desire to abuse or kill.

Animals' egos drive them to fight for prey or territory or to dominate the herd, but the human ego has a constructive or destructive energy. It has built and destroyed many cities. It drives people to be inventive and creative but also makes them obstructive and destructive. People born with a high ego threshold may become dictators, abusers, and ruthless criminals, and their ego expands with the exposure to more temptations. Their ego belief system tells them to blame others and not to accept feedback and has no feelings for people against their beliefs, thoughts, interests, behaviors, or greed.

The ego always searches for *self*-pleasure; it is driven by the desire to be admired or be loved. It blinds people to their own mental and personal limitations, risk assessment, coping ability, and mistakes, making them unable to forgive their ego enemies' limitations or mistakes. It drives men to have families and children but be irresponsible in raising those children. It also makes people eat or buy more than they need, gamble, watch TV, or spend hours searching the Internet for ego-desirable objects or people.

The insecure ego drives people and nations to use their emotional, physical, psychological, financial, managerial, or military power to abuse their ego enemies. Failure to achieve ego desires represents an "ego injury," which can generate negative emotions of stress, fear, hate, and anger (see diagram 1). These negative emotions create harmful *self*-energy, which impairs impartial thinking, concentration, sleep, productivity, trust, and immunity and can trigger physical and mental illnesses.

The human ego is curious to know everything good and bad within and outside of the universe. This has made the news media industry very successful. If a man lived alone on an island, his ego desire would be limited to surviving hunger and thirst, because that would be all he knew. If he found an apple tree, his ego might drive him to taste the fruit, and if there were more than one apple tree, his ego would be greedy to taste the fruit from all of them.

The human ego is a powerful driving force for personal, cultural, and scientific development and failure. A caveperson's ego desires evolved, and his or her ancestors came to desire faster and more powerful technology. People's insecure, greedy egos drive them to invent more powerful self-security or to have more money, power, titles, love, or sex.

As shown in diagram 1, the ego dominates the human thinking (TEBE) pacemaker. Its desire can be productive or destructive. The former has helped humans progress and build civilizations and technology to reach other planets (top box); the latter has been the main cause of abuse and wars. The human ego prevents people from uniting as one nation. It drives children to hate their siblings if they take their food or toys, and without moral conditioning, it can delete humanity or the superego and make siblings enemies for good.

A sibling with a high ego threshold tends to be dominant or abusive, while the sibling with a low ego threshold may share his or her toys. However, ego programming at childhood can expand or erase the superego, or humanity. Racist beliefs can make the ego abusive. Parents teach their children the ego "desirable" religion, culture, race, traditions, and beliefs. Many children are taught that heaven is an "ego desire" and hell is for "ego enemies." This can make children believe that any person who goes against their beliefs is an ego enemy, a sinner who will end up in hell.

The programming process of children's TEBE, or mind pacemaker, gradually creates a subconscious ego desire and can drive them to practice certain behaviors or rituals to achieve their holy ego desires. It can also destroy their humanity and drive them to subconsciously hate or kill an ego enemy who is against their holy ego desires. If they have no power to confront their ego enemy, they may withdraw or subconsciously reject their ego enemy. If they have power, they may abuse an ego enemy who threatens or interferes with their holy ego desires. The religious ego programming has been one of the main causes of hate, neglect, anger, discrimination, desertion, migration, abuse, homicide, terrorism, and war.

The ego desire is usually stronger than religious belief. Many religious people tend to forget their God for a while when they face the temptations of desirable objects, such as money, power, desirable people, or sex. Some even lose control and may sexually abuse children in their temples. After the "sin," they tend to practice more rituals or make a pilgrimage to their holy land in order to delete their sins and regain their ticket to heaven, or ego desire. In certain cultures, a pilgrimage has become a "sinner's land" and a source of profit from sinners who are unable to control their ego desires, addictions, abuses, or sins.

Most ego desires can be achieved using money, which is why people are usually money-minded. Even when they fall in love, many choose an ego-desirable rich person. Their ego is programmed in childhood to recognize ego-desirable people who have certain physical looks, money, power, titles, or similar backgrounds, beliefs, or religions. Any person interfering with achieving one's ego desire is regarded as an ego threat. If the person has no power to resolve that threat, he or she suffers negative emotions, such as fear, anxiety, hate, and anger (diagram 1, left box). These emotions drive them to abuse themselves or others or to "escape" to pleasurable behavior (diagram 1, bottom box). If they have the power to resolve the ego threat, they may become abusive to the person who caused the threat, or their ego enemy (diagram 1, right box).

Vision is the most beneficial and harmful ego tool. Desiring a certain physical look can drive the human ego to reach many continents within seconds through satellite channels, the Internet, smartphones, and digital media. They may locate their ego-desirable person online and insult the ego enemy in the same social media. People may also travel thousands of miles to meet an ego-desirable person, but their desire may fade away when they see a different desirable person.

Unlike in the jungle, in the city, children and adults are victims of their vision, which expands their greed. Their ego is programmed to be stimulated by people with certain physical looks, behaviors, or lifestyles. Boys may engage with beautiful girls and fail to progress academically. Girls cannot leave home without wearing the proper fashion or makeup to attract boys. Adolescents may lose their willpower and "fall in love" when they see an ego-desirable person or may develop greed and addiction to junk food, alcohol, gambling, or Internet games or develop an ego desire to have tattoos or wear hair bands or high heels.

Adults may lose their willpower if they are tempted by money. Even when they become rich, their ego desire may prevent them from spending money or donating part of their fortune. Any threat to their income represents an ego threat and can trigger stress, uncertainty, and strong negative emotions of fear and anger, which can affect their impartial thinking and sleep and prevent them from accepting their mistakes or considering the situation of their ego enemy.

Discrimination is an ego-pandemic behavior. The egos of most people are programmed by their parents, cultures, or the media to be judgmental about objects, subjects, cultures, physical appearances, lifestyles, social classes, races, skin colors, religions, and sexualities. The programmed ego becomes a subconscious personal belief system, dominating the TEBE pacemaker and causing people to judge others within seconds of meeting them in public or in the media. Employers may subconsciously hate foreign employees but cannot sack them, fearing employment laws. They may use or pay for allies or "institutional power" to harm the reputations of the foreign employees. The latter can lose their legal cases if there are no witnesses or evidence to prove racism or abuse.

Many cases of discrimination, racism, power abuse, and rape are unreported because of fear of stigma, career loss, or lack of witnesses. Additionally, justice is not free. The law in many countries is "money-minded," and the legal market is not affordable for everyone. Winning a court case may require a very expensive legal firm. Certain legal firms can get around the law and save criminals, abusers, rapists, and racist organizations from losing their legal cases. Even after losing, they can pay more for appeals. In many countries, a bigger payment means more justice. Hence, employers continue to abuse their power to harm their ego enemies, who may lose incomes, careers, reputations, and health.

The irony is some legal firms are proud of winning the cases of racists, abusers, and criminals. They publish their winning stories in the media in the name of justice to attract more rich abusers, criminals, and racist organizations to invest in their firms. Some advertise for "no-win, no-fee" deals, but after their clients lose their cases, they make them liable to pay all or part of the damages. In certain countries, the law becomes a powerful tool for greedy people to seek money from or revenge against an ego enemy.

Unlike life in the jungle, "civil prostitution" flourishes in the legal market in the cities. Men and women with ego greed to be rich can divorce their rich partners to have their fortune. They may stay unemployed to get free legal aid or to force their partner to pay their legal expenses. This has created a new generation of "civilized prostitutes." Sadly, a traditional prostitute is not always lucky enough to get money from his or her clients, who have an ego desire to have sex but also have the ego power to insult, abuse, or even kill him or her.

Luckily, the egos of abusive people shrink with old age, fear of death, or terminal illnesses. Arrogant leaders, dictators, and criminals may become depressed when they get old and lose their fortunes, physical power, physical looks, titles, fame, security, or health or contract a debilitating or fatal disease. They may become loyal to God, practicing religious rituals or donating money in order to achieve their final ego desire of "heaven."

Superego

The superego is the caring energy in all animals that helps them survive and avoid extinction. In humans, the superego is the opposite of the ego and represents an energy that drives people to be caring, nursing, content, humble, peaceful, and forgiving and to share with, bond with, protect, or defend others. It is the love energy, free from any personal, racial, religious, political, or financial interest or desire. Even beasts show love, care, and protection toward their newborns, which saves them from extinction. They live in groups or herds, share food or prey, and usually protect each other from danger.

Genetically, siblings are born with different superego thresholds. Children born with high superego thresholds tend to be peaceful and caring, sharing their food or toys with their siblings or peers. The high superego threshold can drive humans to become care givers, donors, and peacemakers and to be faithful, sympathetic, humanitarian people or leaders, content with few resources or limited income. However, regardless of children's inherited instinctive thresholds, without moral discipline, their superegos can be erased by the ego's evil energy. Their environment plays a major part in human ego and superego programming. As the ego expands, the superego shrinks or diminishes.

In the cities, the superego is mainly present between parents and their children and in certain care givers and charity workers. The ego of other charity workers may reject supporting an ego enemy or people from another country, race, or religion. Ego greed for money, pleasure, titles, pride, power, sex, or heaven can delete the superegos of people within the same family or culture. Selfish parents may leave their children home alone, split, divorce, or ignore their responsibility toward their children. Their children may do the same in adulthood, leaving their elderly, frail parents alone for years or for good or may wait for the death of their parents in order to get an inheritance.

The ego always dominates the mind or TEBE pacemaker (the subconscious). Children who grow up in dysfunctional families or corrupt systems or countries build many ego enemies, and after years of emotional, physical, or financial abuse, they may lose hope, trust, and faith in changing their abusers and corrupt people or their systems. Many nations suffer from poverty, inequality, or abuse of human rights, mainly because their corrupt leaders have sacrificed their superegos to the temptations of money, power, or titles.

Leaders in the family (parents), work (employers), or culture (politicians) can play a major part in expanding or shrinking the superego. They are shepherds looking after the sheep, but there are very few leaders can inspire others or provide care and support to their people without greed, personal interest, fraud, or discrimination. Lions' superegos can be expanded, and they can be tamed to be submissive in the circus and show love toward their trainers. Similarly, abusers and criminals can be "tamed" and rehabilitated by the superego power to be caring, responsible, and productive.

Children are physically and emotionally attached to their caring parents, who provide them with comfort and care. Lack of care or discipline or acts of neglect or abuse can expand the ego and delete the superego. The ego is always more powerful than the superego and has a strong hold over people's subconscious thinking. It programs people to be slaves and followers of their culture's selfish habits. Adults are under pressure to have a family regardless of their fitness or capability of being a parent or role model. Rich and poor people have strong ego desires to have children, but not all are competent to look after children. The ego-minded people usually don't admit their failures, and subsequently, more children are born and suffer a lack of care, abuse, or poverty. Many children follow their parents' footsteps and repeat the same mistakes; otherwise, they would be regarded as socially abnormal.

It is not difficult to understand abuse in human history. The ego blinds the superego. Parents have a strong desire to have children, but their neglected children may be programmed to be abusers, criminals, or corrupt leaders and politicians. Many politicians are keen to have fame, money, and a title but are incompetent to lead, are selfish, or are racists. In certain civilized counties, the government charges the owner of the dog who attacks a human, but the same government does not charge the parents who brought up abusers, criminals, or corrupt politicians.

The ego urge to have children is more powerful than their superego. It drives them to have sex and bear children without thinking of their personal and financial ability to look after children for eighteen-plus years. They may blame their children for their own failures or abuse their children's rights and ignore their emotional, financial, and educational needs. Their children may repeat their parents' mistakes. Selfish parental behavior has left human civilization threatened by abusers, criminals, terrorists, and corrupt, racist politicians and leaders.

The superego can also be removed by discriminatory religious leaders, who maintain racist judgments against people of other races and faiths and limit their donations to the followers of their own religion. Nations led by politicians with subconscious discriminatory beliefs against other religions promote discrimination, inequality, ethnic cleansing, abuse of human rights, and wars against their ego enemies.

In contrast, leaders with a strong superego can be inspiring even after death. They can inspire many generations to build schools, hospitals, and hospices and donate money to help poor people. Mahatma Gandhi managed to unite people from different backgrounds without violence and used his nation's resources to build an economy without siphoning money into his own accounts. In contrast, most politicians "fake" superego to win votes in the election. They plan their propaganda and take video opportunities to show their fake concern. They may visit their armed forces in a warzone but ignore the innocent civilians—or their ego enemies—they have killed.

Belief

Belief is the level of trust a being has in its surroundings. It is a basic instinct in all animals; they would not survive if they trusted danger. Belief is linked to ego, feeling, thinking, and behavior. Animals believe in danger when they feel (receive sensory stimuli through the five senses) the danger. They make a rapid judgment—whether to fight or flee in the face of danger. If they lose their feelings, e.g., at sleep, they lose their belief and thinking, and become vulnerable to danger.

Each animal, however, has a unique inherited belief threshold and reacts differently to danger. Cats may confront and fight bigger animals, while birds fly away quickly at sensory stimuli. If cats and birds are brought up together as pets, they "trust" each other and live without fighting, despite their natural instincts. Animals usually trust members of their own species and tend to live and migrate in groups or herds. They rarely kill members of their own herd; human "herds" do.

In the first few weeks of life, infants react to their environments according to their inherited instincts, but they are gradually programmed to "feel" and trust the comfortable or painful objects in their environment. The repeated caring and nursing behavior of the parents is reflective. Infants build a trustful relationship and emotional bonds with their caring parents, and they may cry if they lose their parents for a few minutes. In contrast, children become detached from their parents if the parents are abusive.

At birth, children have no fear of beasts until their senses learn, or feel the pain or "get hurt". Their memory is empty of the images of the beasts, but they are programmed by their family to avoid beasts or by experiences, such as when they are threatened or scared by beasts. The repeated threatening behavior may evolve into stress, fear, phobias, and night terrors. They may acquire different types of phobias (e.g., fear of insects or needles) if they watch a fearful reaction from other people.

In contrast, children brought up around a circus environment are programmed to love or trust beasts and judge them by their ego-belief system as ego-safe or ego-desirable beings. Phobias about beasts, snakes, or spiders are also rare in children brought up in a jungle and trained by their parents to hunt animals.

Infants' egos gradually dominate their TEBE pacemaker and become their personal "ego-belief system." As they grow older, children's egos start to judge objects or people as doubtful or believable, desirable or undesirable, or an ego threat or ego enemy. Gradually, they acquire unique ego expectations, values, and judgments on life that become references for their perceptions and feelings. Each child's ego judges thoughts, information, events, and news differently, and children develop different reactions or "feelings" according to their ego judgments or expectations.

As the human ego is selfish, insecure, paranoid, and distrustful, the ego-belief system is usually biased, generating enemies without a fair trial. The ego blinds people from seeing the whole truth, seeing their mistakes, and accepting their ego enemies' mistakes or the impact of their negative behavior. It can prevent children and adults from communicating, forgiving, caring, appreciating, understanding, acknowledging, or accepting any good point in their ego enemy.

Behavior is reflective, contagious, or stimulating. Children "acquire trust" by watching trusted adults' behavior. They learn trustful and distrustful behavior that makes other children or adults "feel" happy, excited, angry, fearful, or sad. Gradually, their egos judge everything they see, hear, meet, taste, or eat according to their ego expectations and values and save the events in their memory as emotional ego memory.

The human ego is more powerful than any spiritual belief. Although most religions are based on ethical behavior, not all religious people exhibit ethical behavior. The curious, insecure, selfish, and greedy ego prevents people from acting or behaving ethically all the time. They may try to achieve their ego greed secretly, to avoid legal punishment, stigma, or shame. Some religious men who preach ethics may commit actions against their own religion when their personal interests are at risk.

Children brought up by fanatical religious parents or cultures develop a religious ego desire to enter heaven and reject the ego enemy (including people from other religions or atheists) or regard them as sinners who will end up in hell. Their TEBE pacemaker is programmed to be judgmental toward people from other races, cultures, or faiths. They are subconsciously programmed to judge people or peers as either ego enemies or ego friends. In adolescence, children become less dependent on their parents and more influenced by their peers and media. They may start to think outside the box or continue to be followers of their parents' or culture's beliefs.

Many religious people believe in "God," but not all of them share the same God. Some religions reject gods that belong to other faiths and regard people belonging to other faiths or subfaiths or atheists as sinners, who will end up in hell unless they change their own belief. Although their belief becomes a source of comfort for their ego, they feel bad, guilty, sinful, or threatened with going to hell if they change their belief, rituals, or way of life, their "behavior." Some subfaiths promise their followers they will enter heaven by killing people who do not practice their own religion, rituals, way of life, or dress code. Their belief about what is required to enter heaven can drive them to kill their ego enemy without feeling guilty, as they strongly believe in securing a place in heaven. They may also feel proud to show the dead victims, or ego enemies, in the media.

The human ego belief system has not changed, so history repeats itself and is full of wars that were based on racist religious grounds, ego hate, anger, and greed to achieve ego desires (e.g., enter heaven by killing the ego enemy). A very few leaders in history have practiced nondiscriminatory behavior toward other religions.

Regardless of what people believe, every person has a unique ego belief system and different perception of God or a "personal God." People may use their personal God during crises (e.g., to pass an exam or an interview), and they may become reluctant to share their personal God and help the whole human race with their prayers. Some people use their personal God to become rich or famous, to win a lottery or a war, or to have a partner, family, or a job. They may also use their God to be cured of illness or to curse their ego enemies with illness or death. At failure, they may blame their God, and in anger, they may act as God to fulfill their selfish, abusive ego desires.

Some people with religious ego desires are programmed to believe that their religion is superior and their sins (but not their ego enemies' sins) can be forgiven by practicing their holy rituals. They may spend a fortune visiting their holy lands many times a year, neglecting their familial responsibility and wasting money on pilgrimages in order to achieve their holy ego desires. They also may donate money to destroy or kill people from other faiths, whom they consider sinners or "dirt." The irony is that if they donated their pilgrimage money toward good works and to help clean up their cities of corruption, dirt, abuse of human rights, and discrimination, they would be terrific role models for their ego enemies and create a desire among them to follow their belief or religion.

People from certain religions and cultures acquire discriminatory religious behavior from their parents and pass it on to their children. They believe they are holy people, that only their faith is a holy faith, and they deserve a holy land, or heaven, while other humans are sinners or inferior. They are programmed to react subconsciously or verbally, and their ego-belief system judges people based on their background, country, dress code, or behavior as sinners or not. They may use the media to promote hate against their ego enemies. Their children may grow up with a subconscious hatred against people of other faiths, races, or sexual identities.

Religious discriminatory parents are not much different from Nazis. They reject people who do not practice their own beliefs. They spend their lives promoting hate and hostility toward their ego enemies in order to achieve their holy ego desires. After killing their ego enemies, discriminatory religious people claim their faith promotes mercy and forgiveness. It is not difficult to understand why Hitler had a big ego appetite to kill millions of people and why human history is repetitive. Racism has been the main ego desire to develop national parties; political and religious parties; daily racist propaganda; discrimination at school, work, and airport checkpoints; ethnic cleansing; global terrorism; and "cold" and "hot" wars.

Jesus has inspired billions of people with his nonjudgmental moral behavior, but not all of his followers follow his behavior or can accept other religions. Regardless of the religion, the ego has unlimited greed and is potentially dangerous to oneself and others. Without moral discipline, the ego drives children to steal to buy ego-desirable items. In adulthood, the expanding ego desire can supersede rational thinking and drive people to cheat, lie, or emotionally, physically, or sexually abuse their powerless ego enemies. Even within the same family and within the same religion, powerful siblings may abuse the rights of less powerful siblings. The greedy, abusive nature of the human ego can't be stopped by religion or law, as people tend to commit sins or abuse secretly or act as group or allies to evade the law.

Both ego threat and ego injury trigger the ANS (autonomic nervous system) to secrete H/N (hormones and neurotransmitters) during a display of negative emotions. These emotions save painful events in the memory and can harm people's immunity, physical and mental health, and sleep and can destroy the trust and bond between siblings, families, friends, and countries for years or for good.

The ego belief system is linked to emotions/feelings and behavior forming "Taha Thinking Triangle," which can be helpful/abusive not only to others but also to the self. A jungle man may kill and eat animals without washing his hands, while the urban man is programmed to "believe" that without washing his hands "behavior", he "feels" dirty. Hand dirt becomes an ego enemy, and many urbanites are obsessed with buying powerful cleaning products or antiseptics for washing their hands, hair, bodies, clothes, children, homes, cars, and pets. The insecure ego belief system makes people feel guilty if they are not using washing products shown in the media or like their neighbors or friends. Their feelings undermine their trust in themselves or their willpower to resist buying more ego-desirable washing products.

People's ego belief systems can delete religious beliefs when they meet an ego-desirable person. Males' egos are programmed to focus on certain desirable parts of a woman's body. This in turn makes the ego of many women prompt them to wear makeup or sexy clothes. Many women lose the confidence to go out without wearing makeup. Even some religious women wear makeup and tight clothes that enhance their breasts or buttocks. The ego may drive people to have tattoos, piercings, and plastic surgery to become more ego desirable. A strong ego desire can remove people's ability to control their willpower. They may travel hundreds of miles to have casual sex with an ego-desirable person they met in a chat room.

The human ego can blind the law and justice. In the courtroom, justice is based on reviewing evidence and witness statements, but the ego pride and desire to win the case can drive the witnesses, lawyers, defendants, and victims to hide part or all of the truth. Most cases of discrimination, abuse, or rape occur without witnesses or the witnesses are strong allies to the abusers. The ego of the abusers or the witnesses may make them lie under oath in court to protect their ego pride from the stigma or legal punishment or to seek revenge against their ego enemies. Later, they believe their lies. Even some lawyers may delete their superego and convince the judge that the abusers were innocent in order to win the case, win money, or win fame as "excellent lawyers" of abusers.

After winning the court case, the ego pride of the abusers and their lawyers change their doubtful belief into fixed belief or affirmation that their lies in court were true and they would not have won their case if they were not true. Their ego pride would reject listening to, accepting, hearing, or believing any evidence from the victims. Their victims may suffer ego injury or lose their reputation, career, or income. Ironically, in certain countries, the legal market becomes more profitable than music, movies, or porn. The insecure ego drives racist people or employers to pay or use professional organizations to blindly support their discrimination, double standards, or abuse. Legal firms can make huge profits by dealing with such racist employers. They usually publish their "legal abuse" in the media to encourage more racist employers to use their services.

Regardless of human beliefs, people try to build trustful relationships with peers, colleagues, professional organizations, political parties, or gangs to protect them in their abuse or from abuse or to build up a successful career or business. A wife may trust her husband's professional skills but not his faithfulness. She may ignore his unfaithful behavior to avoid divorce or losing income. A judge in racist countries may support racist organizations' abuse of foreign employees to protect his country's pride or to avoid losing his job.

Genetically, children have different personal belief systems, but they are programmed differently in each family and culture. Certain people become obsessed with specific numbers, objects, colors, astronomy, superstitions, celebrities, or people who curse or bless them. Their obsession may evolve into phobias or compulsion with certain rituals or habits, which could disable their personal and social lives. In contrast, people who have a strong belief in their astrologists, spiritual leaders, doctors, or famous healers may be cured by a placebo or a touch offered by their trusted spiritual leader, doctor, or healer. This may reflect the impact of belief on human feelings, immunity, biology and well-being.

Judgmental belief systems change over time. In civilized countries, men become less biased toward women, blacks, the disabled, or homosexuals, who gain more civil rights and political power. Similarly, public health awareness has changed people's ego-belief systems. Smoking has been banned in many public places, and people exercise more than before. In contrast, people with poor willpower cannot resist their ego desire to have money, power, food, or sex. The poor may feel vulnerable and unable to resist taking money from the rich. Poverty impairs people's willpower and can drive children and adults to sell their reputations and their bodies or kill for money. Parents may even give up their children for adoption or sell them to pedophilic tourists.

Emotions

Emotions are groups of instincts present in all mammals that create spontaneous reactions and help them to survive danger and avoid extinction. Emotions in humans are chronic, cumulative, programmed by the ego, and saved in the memory as dormant "emotional thoughts" for decades. These emotional thoughts become sources for people's judgments, feelings, behaviors, relationships, and sexualities.

Children at birth express limited responses (mainly crying) during pain and hunger. They start to smile at external stimulations. In supportive families, children express positive emotions, while those living neglected in orphanages or foster homes without stimulation may behave like autistic children—withdrawn or showing limited positive or negative emotions. In contrast, children brought up in broken, dysfunctional, abusive families express a wide spectrum of negative emotions and behaviors—shyness, shakiness, fearfulness, anxiety, stress, hopelessness, sadness, withdrawal, secretiveness, paranoia, vulnerability, powerlessness, hate, anger, nightmares, nocturnal enuresis (wetting their bed), and speech and eating disorders.

Children save strong life events as "emotional thoughts" in their memories for years, and these thoughts become references for their ego judgments. At adulthood, they remember/relate to people, places, objects, food with like-dislike emotions. Genes, determine personality traits and instinctive thresholds, but environment (people behavior, bonding to parents/care givers, culture, media, early abuse, threats, stressors, and social status) program our inherited emotions, and influence our ego judgment and behavior. A physically abusive father may ignite his son's hatred and anger. As the son can't confront his father or leave home, he might abuse his weaker siblings or may choose peers according to his emotional needs (e.g., a fearful child chooses a soft peer to feel safe with). The ego of the son would judge the father as an ego enemy if the father continues to abuse him. The son gradually saves his ego judgment as cumulative negative emotional thoughts in the memory. At adulthood, if the son gains physical power, he may become physically abusive if his ego is threatened by a weaker peer.

Animals express love and anger, but they rarely kill a member of their own species or herd. Humans are the most emotional social animal. Their emotions last for decades and influence their daily moods, interactions, communications, relationships, careers, and productivity. This may reflect the impact of the ego on conditioning human emotions. Domestic cats and dogs may show love to their caring owner, and they usually cry or escape if they are physically abused by their owners. However, they may come back to their owners after a while. The human ego can drive the son to reject, neglect, or emotionally or physically abuse or even kill his abusive father, and he may never forgive his abusive father even many years after his father's death.

Genes can determine the thresholds of human ego and emotions. Children with high inherited ego and emotional thresholds may show abusive, impulsive behavior and vice versa. However, environment (family, culture, media, time, experience, education, and age) can expand or shrink human genetic thresholds. The family "manufactures" children's emotions and egos, while the culture expands or shrinks them. The emotions of a jungle man don't match the emotions of an urban man. Depression, anorexia, and suicide are more common in modern society than in earlier ones. Each generation acquires different emotional conditioning. Children's emotions don't match adolescents', adults', elderly people's, or a dramatic person's emotions.

In each culture, children's TEBE pacemakers or subconscious minds are programmed by certain levels of positive and negative emotions, and these emotions become a source of their spontaneous reactions, feelings, facial expressions, body language, behavior, and sexuality. Urbanites are conditioned to be conscious of their physical looks and age. The media makes profits by exploiting people's insecure egos and emotions to promote their cosmetic products. In a judgment culture elderly, wrinkled, fat, unattractive, or disabled people may develop negative emotions, lose their confidence, feel unwanted or unattractive, lose their hope of making relationships, or fail to get a job.

Anger is a powerful negative emotion and can be destructive to the self and to others. It is generated mainly by the inability of the ego to accept threat, abuse, damage, injury, shame, stigma, failure, behavior, belief, or financial or personal loss or to forgive the person who abuses the ego. Anger is the main cause of domestic abuse, divorce, dismissal, human conflicts, homicides, and wars.

Every person has a certain genetic threshold for anger, but his or her acquired abusive experiences during childhood are saved as accumulated dormant negative energy. It flares up during ego abuse. Dormant anger is influenced by childhood's programming of the ego. An abusive or dysfunctional family generates angry, disunited siblings with strong ego pride, unable to forgive or forget. Similarly, racist religions generate racist people with hatred and anger toward people from other religions. Their religious wars continue for centuries and only end in the grave.

The main source of human emotions is the autonomic nervous system (ANS), which is an emotional store and connects the central nervous system (CNS) with the heart and the endocrine glands. The ANS is divided into two parts: sympathetic and parasympathetic nervous systems. Both parts control and complement each other during emotional crises. During sex, the parasympathetic system causes arousal, while the sympathetic system ends the arousal through orgasm.

Human emotions are programmed at childhood by the ego judgment as ego desirable, ego undesirable, ego safe, ego threat, or ego enemy. Strong, happy, or abusive life events stimulate the ANS to secrete hormones and neurotransmitters (H/N), which can change the human emotional status within seconds and save these events as dormant emotional thoughts in the memory for years. These emotional thoughts become an ego reference and program the TEBE pacemaker and the ANS to subconsciously react and express dormant emotions in future crises.

Humans acquire a wide range of positive and negative emotions (e.g., love/hate, peace/worry care/abuse, happiness/sadness, laughing/crying, admiring/rejecting, contentment/greed, excitement/boredom). Positive emotions give positive energy and drive people to be active and productive. Negative emotions can impair concentration and rational thinking and disturb moods, sleep, creativity, productivity, and immunity. They can trigger many psychosomatic and mental-health issues.

Behavior has a reflective and stimulating impact on emotions and vice versa. Regardless of their inherited emotional thresholds, children are influenced by the good or bad behavior of their caregivers and are programmed to react accordingly. Instinctively, female animals tend to be more caring and protective toward their newborns than male animals. Subsequently, most newborns survive danger. In humans, children are emotionally attached to their caring mothers. They may hate an abusive mother and never forgive her even after her death.

Human emotions accumulate during childhood and can expand into extreme levels. For example, when facing danger, animals either fight, flee, or freeze, while humans may also faint or develop chronic fears and disorders, such as anxiety, stress, speech disorders, eating disorders, poor self-confidence, etc. Just like anger, hate is triggered by ego threats. Hate can last for a second or for decades and can evolve into anger and abuse of self or others. Humans may hate dead people who abused them or abused their families or their country centuries ago. They may also carry chronic hate toward people from other faiths, races, cultures, or sexual orientations.

At an early age, children are conditioned to express different cultural emotions, facial expressions, and body language. People from different cultures express different amounts of emotion. Some cultures are repressed and tight-lipped full with backstabbing, while others are loud and expressive. Genetically, women are more emotional and tearful than men. This may make women more expressive, faithful, and caring to their newborns than men. Men are conditioned not to express weakness, softness, or tears, while it is acceptable for women to cry or scream in public places. Historically, most dictators, abusers, criminals, and rapists have been men. However, with civil rights and freedoms won, women have started competing with men in jobs, behavior, habits, and emotions.

In liberal cultures, many women are now able to smoke and express their emotions in public places more than they were in the last centuries. However, if women gain equal rights and power like men, will this enable them to build skyscrapers, dams, or civilizations? And will homosexual behavior increase in both genders? Nonetheless, women's emotions can be much more powerful than men's muscles. In certain cultures, women keep complaining of men at work or at home. Even when they choose their desirable male partner, they blame men for their own wrong choices, their own mistakes, and their own negative behavior. They use tears to gain support and allies to undermine, blackmail, or destroy their male colleagues' career, or they may threaten their partners with vicious accusations to gain divorce and a legal settlement.

Regardless of genetic or biological behavior, children living in dysfunctional families express more negative emotions, and they may suffer emotional depravation or "emotional hunger," which is a feeling of loneliness and hunger for love or to be loved. The emotional hunger can impair their self-confidence, communication, mood, willpower, and body language. It can make them vulnerable, shy, shaky, or submissive in front of their abusive peers or ego-desirable people. It may influence their sexuality and drive them to a fantasy world, or they may become submissive to strangers who fulfill their desires. Emotional hunger can fill them with negative energy, which may affect their social interactions, tempers, concentration, and school or work performance and make them susceptible to all types of abuse and antisocial, addictive, or criminal behaviors.

Human behavior and emotions are stimulating. The media stimulates children's emotions in a different spectrum. Children are programmed to relate to political media and movies. They show love and hate to certain politicians, leaders, actors, singers, or dancers. Actors and actresses win global awards for their best performance when their acting stimulates audiences' emotions. Audiences may cry, laugh, panic, feel romantic, or become sexually aroused watching movies. Children gradually become conditioned to choose their favorite movies, fiction, or romantic books. Successful authors stimulate adults' and children's emotions, imaginations, and fantasies in their books. The ego is always searching for pleasure, and the porn industry became a successful market for stimulating sexual emotions.

Although the media can have a positive side in inspiring children to achieve goals or have determination to obtain certain careers or professions, racist media coverage creates chronic negative emotions. The media has programmed many generations to be subconsciously judgmental against their ego enemies from certain races, religions, or cultures. People generate negative emotions on a daily basis when they see, watch, or hear their ego enemies in action. Their chronic negative emotions can override their impartial thinking, superego, and humanity and are one of the main causes for human conflicts on this planet. Ironically, the human ego and news have not changed for centuries, but people keep wasting time, money, and energy watching racist news that provokes negative emotions and keeps them insecure, distrustful, and disunited.

Many children are emotionally programmed by watching racist drama, bad language, violence, racist news, or religious programs. Their TEBE pacemaker is conditioned to subconsciously react with negative emotions toward ego enemies. In contrast, watching comedies or scientific or humanities programs can inspire children with positive emotions, ambitions, and energy to be caring or creative.

People can fake emotions for personal, financial, or political reasons, and it may be difficult to trust strangers. A politician may fake loyalty to win an election, and a prostitute can fake orgasm to win over clients. In interviews and blind dates, people who show positive emotions may win a job or love, respectively. However, people cannot hide their extreme emotions of fear, anger, or happiness at winning money or passing an exam.

Sex is an instinctive and emotional behavior, associated with love or submission. Family, culture, and the media program people to subconsciously emotionally react to certain ego-desirable people. The emotions of love, romance, and sexual desire can be a sedative, impairing people's rational thinking and preventing them from making wise judgments. They may have sex without protection or without using condoms and acquire STDs/HIV, or they may end up with children and fail to share responsibility for them.

Feelings

Feelings are different from emotions, as they represent a "conscious" reaction of our programmed instincts toward external sensory stimuli received by the five senses or retrieved from the memory, while emotions represent conscious, subconscious, and unconscious internal impulses expressed by our programmed instincts. We lose feeling when we lose our five senses (e.g., during sleep), but our emotions may continue during sleep and we may wake up with hunger pains, thirst, nightmares, sweating, or the urge to urinate, and after puberty, boys may develop erections and have nocturnal ejaculations during sleep, without conscious physical or sexual contact or feeling.

Animals usually maintain the same instinctive feelings all the time (apart from domestic animals), while human feelings evolve gradually after birth from instinctive into acquired or cultural feelings, which change with time. A caveperson's feeling is usually instinctive while a modern person acquires diverse feelings.

After leaving the dark environment of the womb, newborns begin their life journey. They start receiving life stimuli though their five senses and start to "feel life". They face different sensory stimuli from family, culture, or media. Initially, they react according to their inherited instinctive thresholds. Gradually, both thinking and emotions are largely influenced by the programming of the ego during childhood, which becomes a personal belief system, controlling the TEBE pacemaker and the ANS to react subconsciously to the surrounding events, generating positive and negative ego judgments, which influence people's feelings.

Feeling has a major impact on human daily behavior and vice versa. We go to bed, wake up in the morning, go to work, go on holiday, or go to court, with different good and bad feelings. An actor, singer, or leader may win millions of people's hearts if he or she is able to make them feel good, while a dictator generates hatred among people. Feelings of worry or fear restrict people's daily behavior, and feelings of anger have major negative impacts on human history, creating abuse and wars. Feelings of failure, loss, hopelessness, stigma, or shame can lead to depression and/or suicide.

Happy feeling can charge people with powerful energy. They may feel over the moon when they win money, prize, pass an exam, get a degree, get a profitable job, or fall in love. The erotic feeling of sex can make men addicted to sex, masturbation, or porn. The media acts on people's feelings to make massive profits through commercial ads, movies, sports, music, and news. National propaganda can brainwash millions of people to make them feel angry about a person or a nation's behavior, religion, or traditions.

Children are born with different inherited emotional thresholds and generate different reactions after birth. They react differently toward pain, fear, and abuse. Their inherited thresholds, however, gradually shrink or expand according to cultural norms (traditions, law, media, and religions) and the type of support, temptations, neglect or abuse available in their environment. At birth, newborns react spontaneously to sensory stimuli, such as light, hunger, or pain, but their perceptions, expectations, reactions, or feelings gradually change according to the cultural norms.

Children born in the jungle are exposed to limited temptations, education, cultural values, or expectations. They acquire limited ego greed and develop limited feeling spectra, emotional swings, and mental illnesses. In the city, children gain a wide spectrum of temptations and develop high expectations, greed, desires, and enemies. They learn social classes, rich and poor; cultural good and bad behavior; and cultural preferences for attractive people, cars, jobs, careers, education, holidays, hobbies, furniture, and electrical and digital equipment. Their happy feeling is influenced by having the best of their cultural values (e.g., the best house, car, gadgets, food, or clothes). In contrast, the happy feelings of cavepeople may include hunting and eating prey.

Feelings are influenced by beliefs, ego judgments, thinking, and behavior. A caveperson can't feel doubt or things he or she can't see, hear, touch, smell, or taste, e.g., God. However, his or her ego needs for support during crises can drive him or her to search, think, in the doubt for a savior that gives him or her safe feelings for his or her insecure ego. Ego belief in God can make him or her feel safe or comfortable and can drive him or her to be caring, helping the others. However, when his or her greedy ego faces new desires or enemies, he or she may ignore God for a while, until he or she finishes his or her ego greed. If he or she acquires a racist religion, he or she may curse, bully, abuse, torture, or kill his or her ego enemy.

During history, people believed in different types of gods (e.g., fire, water, sun, evil, or animal), and their beliefs have influenced their feelings and behaviors. Their ego belief system may be programmed at childhood to judge belief in God as holy and safe, a saving divine power. Their ego judgment gives them a comfortable feeling when they pray or obey God and can expand their superego's behavior, but the selfish, greedy and abusive nature of the human ego is more powerful than religion. It can drive people to argue, fight, and abuse each other even within the same religion.

Behavior is stimulating and reflective of human feeling. At birth, children have no phobias, no fears of height, elevators, snakes, or spiders, until they learn or their feelings get hurt. They may be threatened with fearful objects and develop phobias from these objects. The powerless children who are unable to confront the person who threatens them may save the threatening events in their memories for years as dormant, fearful events, or emotional thoughts, which influence their behaviors, feelings, performance, health, and sleep. In contrast, children in the jungle may be encouraged to hunt beasts and not to be threatened by them. Parents' love and support make children feel happy, confident, or brave, while abusive parents expand the feelings of hate and fear, which can provoke angry thoughts and behaviors in their children for years.

With exposure to cultural and media events, children's egos start to make judgments and a long list of preferences (ego desires and ego enemies) and react, or feel, according to ego expectations in negative or positive directions, programming the

TEBE pacemaker to subconsciously react toward cultural values, e.g., best country, leaders, religion, job, or movie star. Children also learn the bad, ugly, painful, or fearful objects. These ego values become affirmations for their personal belief system and their egos start to subconsciously judge life events and fuel the self with negative or positive feelings, or energies, which influence their behavior.

As money, power, pleasure, abuse, love, or sex is the main source for ego desire, it is also the source of good feelings in many cultures. Money is one of the main powerful factors that influence people's behaviors, moods, or feelings. They are programmed at an early age to become rich or develop dreams to have profitable jobs. Poor people may migrate to rich countries or marry rich people to feel secure. Poor children may feel bad, emotionally deprived, or inferior if they cannot buy what their peers have. Their feelings fuel them with negative energy (hate, envy, or anger) or undermine their confidence and make them feel inferior, submissive, and vulnerable to the abuse of rich peers or strangers who offer them attention, money, or gifts.

Even rich urbanites may feel insecure without investments. Their greedy ego feels vulnerable to loss if they donate money to the poor or to charities. They may have difficulty trusting people or may develop paranoia that people are after their money. They may suffer severe stress, chronic anxiety, or insomnia or become seriously ill after losing their fortunes. Their stress triggers the ANS or emotional store to secrete negative emotions for days, which can trigger serious medical or psychological illnesses. In contrast, people are conditioned to feel good when they have the attention or support of an ego-desirable person (rich, powerful, or attractive).

Feelings can divide humans into leaders and followers or independent and dependent. Followers can't live alone and feel insecure without following their cultural traditions, lifestyles, habits, fashions, gossip, rumors, or backstabbing ways, while leaders are confident, content, rational, wise, creative, thoughtful, and independent. They lead themselves and/or are able to inspire people to follow them.

Food has become a source of comfort feelings in modern society. People tend to eat when they are alone or when they feel bored, stressed, happy, or excited. Children and adults feel hungry when they see delicious food, sweets, or junk food. They tend to think of food or eat even if they are full. Some become obsessed with junk food and cannot leave their desirable food in their fridge for long without needing to have "a bite." In contrast, children who live in the jungle may never develop an obsession with junk food not available in their environment (e.g. ice cream).

Food is the main cause of pandemic obesity and its comorbidities, such as diabetes, arthritis, poor mobility, high cholesterol, high blood pressure, heart disease, heart attack, and stroke, bleeding patients' and health care's budgets. Some people feel guilty after eating junk food, fearing gaining weight and becoming obese or sexually undesirable. After gaining weight, they may try to lose weight to feel good, attractive, or sexy. Their ego desire for food may undermine their willpower to resist eating food, and some of them many suffer from bulimia or anorexia.

Feelings are reflective. Happy teachers inspire students to be creative, while boring teachers can make students hate school. Abusive leaders can drive people to change jobs, cities, or countries. During a job interview, people tend to choose a candidate who makes them feel happy, confident, or trustful. At work or in public places, people's egos are programmed to choose a person who has certain physical looks and behaviors that make them feel good. Good feelings can improve immunity and mental illnesses. Happiness makes people feel younger and productive, while sadness makes them feel weak, tired or old. Getting old or wrinkled can make people feel unattractive and may drive some to have plastic surgery.

Feelings can't be easily deleted, as they are dominated by the ego belief system. People may live with their past feelings for years or for good. They may never forgive their ego enemies or their abusive parents, partners, siblings, teachers, peers, employers, or leaders. Some people with homosexual feelings may never get rid of them, and this can make them feel guilty, ashamed, rejected, sinful, or unable to marry, perform heterosexual sex, or have children. Their chronic feelings can damage their willpower to be normal like others and may drive them to commit suicide.

Changing human feelings is a difficult or impossible task, as it requires changing the ego belief system or the way of thinking. Most human feeling is acquired by early childhood learning and conditioning experiences. Changing the way of thinking can help to overcome negative feelings. During meditation, people may lose their five senses and dive into a peaceful space but only for a short time. Accepting our own mistakes, accepting the worst news or results, undermining the source of fear, pleasure, anger or pain, keeping a positive attitude, practicing positive activities, changing the environment, or relationships, skipping past negative thoughts or the sources of negative feelings, (e.g., political media, drama, negative songs, singers, performers, presenters, or programs) can help to change people feeling.

People can fake their feelings at home, work, or in the media. They may laugh at work but feel low at home. They may cry in court to gain a judge's sympathy. Men can fake romance with their wives after committing adultery. They can sleep and have sex with their wives, but their sexual feelings are with someone else who makes them "feel" sexually aroused to achieve orgasm. Politicians can fake their feelings of humanity to win more votes, and porn stars may fake their orgasm noises to win more money or fame. However, people can't easily hide their feelings during crises or extreme emotions, such as panic, phobia, anger, orgasm, or joy from winning the lottery.

Learning

Learning is an instinct that helps animals survive hunger and danger. They learn where to find or hide food. Learning is a more advanced instinct in humans. They are able to acquire facts, information, knowledge, skills, experiences, training, education, and academic degrees and be professionals or scientists. Science is a continuous chain of learning, starting with first human generation to invent the wheel and ending with the death of the last human on earth.

Learning has a major impact on programming human behavior in positive or negative ways. It starts when a mother stimulates her newborn to talk, smile, or sing. Infants learn how to drink, eat, talk, sit, walk, greet, or behave according to their family and cultural traditions. Culture can inspire children to become professionals or creators. It can also make them judgmental, fanatics, racists, abusers, or criminals. Many learned skills and behaviors remain permanent for life and cannot be easily deleted from memory, such as reading, writing, talking, walking, swimming, driving, language, body language, facial expressions, voice tone, or communication style.

Learning is influenced by the inherited IQ levels, interests, and competency of other sanity elements, particularly the ego. The ego can make children keen to learn and develop goals in life but can also make them unproductive or abusive. The brain has unlimited potential to learn everything in the universe, but the ego has certain interests, desires, and enemies that form barriers and threats to rapid scientific progress over the last centuries. The ego can be influenced by temptations, support, motivation, greed, abuse, failure, belief, threats, pride injuries, fears, anger, poverty, and cultural values.

Additionally, the ego can't survive without pleasure or abuse. Humans can't study or work continuously without having a break or fun, and sometimes, they abuse others for hours or centuries. It took Stone Age humans many centuries to unit to invent digital technology, and although such technology has improved and accelerated scientific progress, the ego may spend hours online looking for desirable programs, games, gambling, fashions, movies, music, sports, dating agents, chat rooms, and sex or tend to abuse its ego enemies in social media.

However, without the greedy human ego, the Stone Age people might not have progressed scientifically. The ego drove the jungle people to build civilizations, but its insecurity can be destructive. Environment has a major impact on the ego. Despite the fact that we are born with different inherited thresholds for learning, family, culture, and media influence our learning opportunities. Dysfunctional families, poverty, fanatical beliefs, and emotional, physical, financial, and sexual abuse can affect children's learning and school performance. Even children with high IQs may not develop their talents if they are not offered the opportunity to learn. In contrast, dyslexic or disabled children might obtain a PhD if they are offered support and opportunities for academic education.

Culture manufactures people's mentalities, beliefs, and education levels more than genes. It pollutes the inherited learning capacity with mental barriers. In competitive, rich societies, children from supportive families have an opportunity to progress to high academic levels and generate competitive technology. In corrupt cultures, children may follow their corrupt system or migrate to obtain education. Many countries suffer from poverty, corruption, inequality, bias, fanatical beliefs, and abuses of civil rights. They recycle the same model of human beings with similar fanatic beliefs. Fanatics may gain high academic degrees, but their ego-belief system can make them unable to be creative, work professionally, or progress scientifically.

Fanatical parents teach their children to reject certain behaviors, religions, races, or ethnicities. Their children save the fanatical beliefs as dormant emotional thoughts in their memories for years, which hypnotizes their mind pacemaker to reject or ban freedom of expression against their holy thoughts. Subsequently, their cultures lack peace, stability, equality, human rights, and scientific and economic progress. Their ego desire is always more powerful than their religion. Although they tend to reject their ego enemies' religion, they may ignore their own religious ethics through greed for money, power, title, pleasure or sex and are totally dependent on their enemies' technology and exports of food, alcohol, tobacco, drugs, health equipment, transport, academic books, construction, internal security, digital technology, sewing needle, baby food, fashion, makeup, movies, porn, sex toys, and military forces.

Learning from mistakes can be difficult and painful. The ego pride and greed prevent humans from accepting their mistakes. The ego drives people to have a relationship with an ego-desirable person without thinking of the risks involved. After the desire fades, they discover the negative or the abusive nature of the ego-desirable person. However, their ego pride refuses to admit its mistake of choosing the wrong person. The ego greed and pride also prevents people from admitting their abuse or mistakes to others. Abusive employers or leaders tend to blame and criticize their employees or others instead of fixing their mistakes and being role models.

Academic learning enables people to analyze, criticize, and judge life facts or research more objectively and differentiate between scientific facts and fiction, but human ego tends to be biased in its judgment. Some scientists make judgments based on their ego-belief systems, or they may do research in order to gain fame, title, prize or funding. The egos of many people including scientists may make strong judgments that God does not exist, but science can't deny facts or hypothesis without evidence.

Learning may be impaired by tiredness, illness, narcotics, or alcohol and may be gradually diminished by dementia. Cultural learning in early childhood crafts certain human models with specific body language, accent and behavior, which may not be acceptable by other culture. People in racist countries accuse foreign employees that they don't listen and/or change their behavior according to their own wishes, yet they reject to be accused by the same accusations.

Understanding

Understanding is the ability to listen, receive, perceive, anticipate, predict, analyze, interpret, solve, or answer a question, life fact or to improve insight and behavior. Understanding is a key issue in learning, intelligence, and progress. It is an instinct that helps people survive and progress. Human understanding is also influenced by the ego, which can drive people to invent, create, or abuse. Ego threats can prevent people from understanding and solving problems in a rational way (see diagram 1).

Genetically, not all people understand information the same way or give the same answers in exams. Science would not progress if we had identical understanding abilities. Creative people understand and perceive things differently and are able to make interpretations, offer explanations, or invent new technologies and create art or literature. Academic education can improve our knowledge and understanding, but the ego desire for power, money, pleasure, abuse, or revenge may prevent us from realizing academic progress.

Anger resulting from ego injury can form a blind spot in the human mind, distracting people from understanding how their risky behavior can be harmful to themselves or others. The mind's blind spot can expand or shrink according to the programming of the mind pacemaker and the support people have in their environment. Urbanites are conditioned to be judgmental, and their ego judgments can impair their risk assessment, or understanding of their ego enemies. The ego judgment can affect their daily communication, career, income, personal lives and fate.

Fanatic belief is also creates blind spots, barriers, and difficulty in understanding people, nature, magic, illusions, facts, secrets, truth, or things beyond the universe. Similarly, the urban ego is programmed to be blind or interested in money, power abuse, authority, fame, title, physical looks, or the size of sex organs rather than the size of the universe. People may have difficulty understanding a question addressed to them by an ego-desirable person. Their eyes and mind focus on the ego-desirable part of the human body.

The human ego is programmed to be emotionally or sexually aroused when meeting a desirable person. This may block the person's understanding. After forming a relationship or being married for months or years, their ego desires may fade away, and they may discover that they can't understand each other. Their "ego lover" becomes an ego enemy or ego threat to their freedom or finances. The threat can trigger the TEBE pacemaker to release negative emotions, which can impair understanding and objective thinking (see diagram 1).

The language barrier is an important factor in failing to understand foreign people or cultures. We cannot understand errors when we read foreign languages, and we fail to pass exams in foreign languages without prior learning. In contrast, an ego determination to create, invent, or be rich or famous can drive people to migrate, learn a new language, and compete with the native or foreign people in their careers, inventions, or contributions.

The five senses can affect people's understanding. Without sign language, deaf people might not understand verbal information, and without touch, many blind people would be unable to understand shapes or sizes of objects. Receiving multiple sensory stimuli at the same time may impair our understanding. Listening to music and the TV at the same time impairs our understanding capacity.

Powerful emotions can also impair our understanding. During stress, anger, or fear, people are often unable to understand what they have been told. Misunderstanding is a global communication problem. It can be associated with ego perception, expectations, interests, values, mental status, age, sex, personal beliefs, social background, or mental programming.

People's understanding is programmed to certain traditions, values, behaviors, beliefs, dress codes, habits, rituals, media cultures, or propaganda. Some people understand information differently or perceive news according to their ego-emotional judgment. They may become bulimic or anorexic when they receive media information on the obesity risk, or they may become obese and blame the fast-food industry.

Racist beliefs can make people misunderstand their ego enemies. They tend to make rapid, wrong judgments based on the physical looks, skin color, language, body language, facial expressions, attitudes, and dress codes of people from other cultures. Their misunderstanding can create daily conflicts, abuse, and "cold wars." Misunderstanding of scientific research can lead to a disaster, such as inventing harmful, teratogenic or carcinogen drugs or weapons.

Behavior

Behavior includes all the physical, mental, conscious, subconscious, and unconscious reactions and energy or activities expressed during wake and sleep. Any action can induce counteraction and behavior is the outcome of the reaction between the genes and the environment (family, culture and media). Human behavior is one of the most important markers for human personality, intelligence, credibility, mentality, competence, masculinity or femininity with certain culture.

Animals in different countries express similar instinctive behaviors, while humans behave differently in each culture. Culture manufactures many aspects of human behavior, self-identity, intellect, ethics, mentality, beliefs, emotions, reactions, interactions, body language, voice tones, accents, sexual behaviors, and sexuality. Behavior can help one recognize an Indian from a Chinese or African person. It also differentiates sane versus insane, extrovert versus introvert, shy versus brave, peaceful versus abusive, leader versus follower, and live versus dead.

Genetically, each sibling behaves differently after birth. Even identical twins have different behaviors, and their behavior becomes more diverse if they are brought up from birth in different cultures and different religions. Almost all religions focus on moral behavior, but behavior is not always influenced by a religion. Environment pollutes human genetic or instinctive behaviors in each culture differently. Most human behavior is acquired or manufactured by the family, culture, and media rather than by genes. Genes determine people's physical looks, physical power, gender, personality traits, ego and emotional thresholds, and diseases. However, genes don't determine the type of culture, care, education, media, temptations, abuse, sexual experience, infections, traumas, accidents, crises, we have after birth.

Infants are born without qualifications, bank accounts, sexual partners, careers, degrees, awards, or criminal records. They don't choose their family, culture, country, or time period. Their inherited genetic behavior gradually expands or shrinks with the environment. A Stone Age man had different behavior than a modern urbanite has, and the time affects people's behaviors. Adam would not react with love or anger if he was created alone. His behavior would change when he met Eve or abusive men. He might fight the abusive men if he felt powerful, or he might make friendships, alliances, or a tribe with them. Human history has changed from tribes to cultures and nations, but their insecure egos have kept them as followers, "prisoners" of their roles, traditions, habits, laws, beliefs, taboos, systems, social classes, economies, dress codes, borders, visas, and flags. Any behavior against the traditions may be regarded as shameful, odd, illegal or sinful.

Certain cultures manufacture technology; other cultures manufacture fat people or both. Conditioning in cultural traditions influences people's daily behaviors, thoughts, feelings, and emotions. Their behavior pollution may start in the womb or in their mother's environment. The embryo is affected by the mother's medical and psychological status. Her negative and positive emotions could affect her immune system, hormones, and her newborn's health. Drugs, smoking, and alcohol may also affect the newborn's behavior, growth, and health. After birth, infants express different inherited traits and interests. However, parents and culture determine people's fates. Genes do not teach children language, science, religion, beliefs, rituals, or abusive or antisocial behaviors—parents and cultures do.

People are programmed to follow "acceptable" cultural traditions at home, work, and in public places. In the past, men were expected to be in charge of the family's expenses and critical decisions, while women were expected to look after the home and the children. Now, both parents may work and share family responsibility. However, despite women's financial independence, urban cultures still don't accept women sexually harassing men in the street or marrying a homeless man. Women are also under cultural pressure to get married and have children before menopause. With more cultural and civil freedoms, men's and women's behaviors have started to change, and many formerly unacceptable or shameful behaviors have become acceptable. It became acceptable for men and women in Western cultures to have homosexual relationships and adopt children. Euthanasia is legalized in certain countries, as is abortion.

Behavior stimulates feelings, and feelings stimulate behavior. Caring supportive behavior can build a powerful trust and makes us "feel good" or confident. It can improve our attitude and performance. Happy, loving parents raise happy, confident children. Incompetent, unloving parents bring up unhappy, vulnerable children. Teachers can inspire students to be professional or drive them to hate or leave school. Nations respecting human rights keep their citizens loyal and proud of their countries, while dictators generate rebels, abusers, and victims of abuse. Spiritual or religious leaders' behavior can have "magical" or hypnotic effects on the human mind. It can make millions of people productive, destructive, or racist.

People's behavior is influenced by their culturally programmed ego-belief system or ego judgment. In many cultures, people judge themselves by their behavior, country, religion, age, dress code, skin, eye or hair color, physical looks, breast size, or buttock size. The human ego can't survive without pleasure, greed, abuse, or pride. Even some religious people evade their holy religious roles for their ego desires. Their religion may recommend following certain moral behaviors, ethics, rituals, and dress codes and ban immoral behavior and sexual relationships outside marriage, but their ego desires, greed, and pride drive them to lie, cheat, or steal to fulfill their ego wishes. They may skip their religious roles if the civil law provides them with more money than their religious roles do.

During childhood, most human behavior is learned and programmed in the TEBE pacemaker as dormant emotional thoughts and saved in the memory as subconscious files. Families program children's emotions, while cultures shrink or expand people's egos and emotional behavior. Emotional programming during childhood crafts specific expressions and body language in each person. Love, care, education, and supportive discipline give children trust, ego comfort, confidence, and emotional independence while abuse drives them to counterabusive behavior, aggression, isolation, or emotional dependence with dysfunctional ego hunger for love, support, abuse or to be abused.

In adulthood, facial expressions are conditioned by the emotions people acquired and saved in their subconscious minds during childhood. While looking at photos, we may feel the emotions behind the facial expressions. Meeting or working with them gives us a better understanding of their personalities and behavior. However, the real personality can't be assessed without living with a person. People's egos drive them to hide their desires, secrets, and greed in public places, such as work, in social media, on job interviews, or on a blind date.

The insecure, greedy, and distrustful human ego has not changed since the beginning of time and has disunited and separated people in their houses, countries, and along their borders. Even loving couples who lived together for decades may split up when their egos come under threat. Any threat to people's ego desires, greed, or pride can drive loving couples, siblings, peers, neighbors, and nations to split up. The threat can also drive them to abuse their ego enemies in the family, street, at work, or during war. The ego has made mankind the most constructive and destructive beast to the environment.

In each culture, there are certain acceptable behaviors for each place, time, and gender. People can't laugh or dance in the street if they are attending a funeral. They can't express their love or hate to a stranger in public places unless they have the power to do so. Each culture has certain roles and limitations. While watching different movies, we may recognize the type of culture from the behavior of the actors and actresses.

There is no "normal" human culture in developed or developing cultures, but there are acceptable and unacceptable behaviors. Every culture has different acceptable social behaviors, and people's behavior changes with the times. Discrimination on the basis of sex, race, religion, disability, and sexuality has become unacceptable in many civilized cultures. People's attitude toward human rights, freedom, sex, abortion, children's welfare, and healthy habits are also changing in civilized cultures. In male-biased cultures, it is acceptable for males to be abusive and irresponsible, neglecting their families and children, and unacceptable for men to be weak, soft, honest, polite, productive, or professional. There are also acceptable and unacceptable behaviors and dress codes for both sexes in every country.

In civilized nations or in the jungle, "group power" has been the most *acceptable* type of power in human history. Groups of people or nations can lobby together and commit different types of abusive, unacceptable, immoral, or criminal actions and may evade the law. The lobbying of powerful politicians or countries can determine the lives of millions of people during peace or wartime. People's demonstrations and campaigns can change civil laws. Even groups of professionals, such as doctors or lawyers, can lie in court to abuse their ego enemies and evade the law.

Children are powerless and have no choice but to follow their cultural norms to avoid punishment or shame. At school, they discover new behaviors by observing peers or teachers. They are exposed to the media and develop curiosity and interest in certain ego-desirable behaviors. They may experiment certain adult behaviors. The ego always searches for self-pleasure, and pleasurable behavior is addictive, particularly at an early age. Without support and discipline, children may become addicted to certain behaviors or habits, such as smoking, drinking alcohol, or masturbation.

In the cities, many adolescents are followers of their peers' "cool" behavior or lifestyle choices, such as smoking, drinking alcohol, using illicit drugs, bullying, copying celebrities' fashions, getting tattoos or piercings, or experimenting with sexual behaviors. In adulthood, people comply with their work environment, culture, roles, guidelines, discipline, and policies. In civilized cultures, people's behavior is influenced by legal punishment. In corrupt cultures, people are followers of their corrupt system. In both cultures, human egos may expand, driving people to be emotional, selfish, insecure, moody, partial, secretive, money-minded, greedy, judgmental, abusive, unreliable, promiscuous, and distrustful.

Culture pollutes human instinctive behavior and humans pollute the environment with pesticides, emissions of gases, nuclear waste products, political propaganda, media noise, wars, and destruction. Their insecurity left them separated in "cages" (homes) where they can live and sleep without the fear of theft or being killed. Even at home, humans have to maintain certain behaviors with their family; otherwise, separation or divorce may ruin the family unit.

Changing human behavior is nearly impossible after childhood, as children's negative emotions are saved in their memories for decades and become part of their invisible or "dormant" subconscious behaviors. Parents are usually the first caregivers or abusers of children's emotions. They are the first child abusers if they are incapable of looking after their children's moral, emotional, financial, and educational needs.

The diversity of human behavior is recognized in history books and in the daily newspapers or media. The media shows people caring—they support, donate, invent, and create—but also shows people committing crimes and abuses on a daily basis all over the world. In return, the media uses ego curiosity and insecurity to have provocative effects on human behavior. It has programmed people's egos with news, movies, fashions, and vanity shows. People are concerned about their physical looks, security, and income. Political propaganda and commercial media become a "noise pollution" acting on human ego desires and ego enemies. The political media make certain cultures an ego enemy, but other media (e.g., travel ads) can make the same culture seem like heaven on earth.

Based on economic status, behavior, and lifestyle, urbanites have been divided into three or more social classes: lower, middle, and upper. Each class has different traditions, values, mentalities, morbidities, and mortalities. The gap is wide between the upper and lower classes in the way they communicate, such as through their voice tones, accents, facial expressions, and body language. The upper class may feel insecure mixing with the lower class, and the lower class may "upgrade" their social status if they gain fortune, but they usually keep expressing their common behavior.

Society's behavior is influenced by economy, leadership, politics, traditions, laws, religions, or beliefs. Civilized countries made progress in different aspects of life, as their citizens are conditioned to respect the law and human rights at work or in public places. However, they may make profits selling military weapons to corrupt nations, which may use weapons for terrorism against the civilized counties that sold the weapons to them. Many corrupt countries have not progressed for decades because they keep recycling their corrupt behavior or fanatical beliefs for many centuries. Their corrupt cultural behavior and beliefs lack equality, freedom of expression, or simple human rights. They generate abusers and victims of abuse, who may migrate with the birds searching for a better environment.

Behavior and Fear

Fear is an instinct that protects humans and animals from danger. Animals may fight or flee when facing danger. They usually defend themselves or try to escape death. Humans may react in a similar way but may also collapse, faint, or be submissive to the abuser or killer. Fear in childhood is saved in the memory as dormant emotional thoughts, which become references for future behavior or chronic negative emotions, such as social shyness, embarrassment, avoidance behavior, stress, anxiety, phobias, panic, guilt, hate, aggression, or anger. Most fears are acquired in childhood as dormant fearful emotional thoughts, which program the TEBE pacemaker to subconsciously react to fearful events with rational or irrational behavior.

Newborns do not fear pain until their instincts (genes) get hurt. First, their egos learn the safe and unsafe object and their instincts react (emotions) to the external sources of the pain received by the five senses generating (feeling), and then their TEBE pacemaker becomes programmed with emotional fearful thoughts, which are saved as dormant uncomfortable or painful files in their memories. Almost all human conflicts start with "sensory abuse," or abuse of human feelings, by certain unacceptable behavior, which hurts others' feelings. Children's abuse can program their minds with fearful emotional thoughts for years, affecting their daily performance, confidence, body language, social interaction, and sexuality. In contrast, spoiled children raised without discipline may also develop fear of facing life crises without support from their parents, relatives, or peers.

Accumulated fearful subconscious thoughts retreat and then flare-up during stress or ego conflict as acute emotional behavior. Fear can trigger many negative emotions (see diagram 1). These emotions form a negative mental energy that can be expressed as hate, depression, anxiety, anger, or hostility, and if the ego conflict isn't solved, it can lead to psychosomatic disorders and mental illnesses affecting all aspects of people's lives.

Culture is dominated by ego power. The ego of powerful siblings makes them tend to abuse their weaker brothers and sisters. Powerful people's or nations' egos can make them tend to abuse weaker people or countries. Ego power can be gained by money and titles, and people tend to make allies with rich, powerful, or professional people, just as weak nations tend to make allies with powerful nations to protect their interests. Many women are attracted to powerful men, and many muscular men become submissive to their dominant wives. Their insecure ego fears life without personal or financial protection.

Fear limits human behavior. Without fear, people would express their feelings, emotions, secrets, savings accounts, sexual desires, sexual orientations, sins, or crimes to each other, and they may commit any unacceptable, shameful, or criminal behavior on a daily basis. Fear of the law can prevent people from committing visible crimes, but it cannot stop their ego greed or "invisible" human abuse. People may commit adultery, abuse, rape, or murder in secret to evade the law. Similarly, group power can evade the law by uniting under the umbrella of a national society or a party. Groups of doctors, lawyers, politicians, or terrorists can unite to abuse their less-powerful ego enemies.

As behavior is stimulating and reflective, children may develop the same phobias as their parents or siblings. Repeated viewing of fearful behaviors can condition their TEBE to react in a similar way. This is more common in genetically and emotionally susceptible children who are born into dysfunctional families or with an obsessive-compulsive disorder (OCD) or trait. In contrast, happiness can quickly resolve fearful and painful events and illnesses. Winning the lottery can delete all the negative symptoms and pain and may cure many psychosomatic and mental illnesses.

Fear of hell may deter religious people from committing crimes or abuse but may also make them feel guilty, obsessively repeating their religious rituals after each sin they commit. Obsession with fear may limit their rational thinking, sleep, social interaction, and productivity. Similarly, fear from taboos or STDs may limit people's sexual behavior. In contrast, fear can be a source of sexual arousal or excitement in masochists and sadists, who enjoy violent or abusive sexual behavior without love or emotion. The thrill of adrenaline resulting from fear can also push many people to watch horror movies or ride roller coasters. Action movies become a source of entertainment, and the more torture, abuse, and killing in the movie, the more people's egos are curious to watch.

Money is an ego tool for pleasure, power, security, and fame. The fear of being poor or losing money has made many people insecure, depressed, or obsessed with saving money and careful in their expenditures. The ego greed drives some of them to divorce their partners to gain money or to secure income after divorce. Even when they become rich, they may look for more investments and wealth and may become upset if they lose assets or face an ego threat. Failing to achieve ego desires or financial security can provoke many negative emotions, which can affect their relationships, family life, or their children's lives. In contrast, lack of fear can have a negative impact on human behavior. Spoiled children who grow up without fear and moral discipline may become dependent, moody, superficial, impulsive, or abusive, with no goals or ambitions in life. In certain cultures, fear of getting fat may cause bulimia and anorexia, while people in poor cultures fear death from starvation.

Treatment of fear-related emotions and disorders, such as anxiety, stress, guilt, shyness, hate, anger, insomnia, nightmares, or phobias, start from within. Most fears are related to ego desires, pride, or greed. Accepting death or the worst thing that could happen from a fearful person or event can kill the ego. Changing the way of subconscious thinking—mind beats—allows one to live each day without thinking or relating to the past or fearful events, e.g., thinking that you are living in an empty environment. The media tend to use the insecure ego, which is liable to addiction to pleasure, power, money, and abuse. It programs children and adults to be receptive, addictive, or submissive to their provocative bias propaganda. Skipping daily political news and replacing TV dramas, racist movies, negative songs, or performers with happy, positive programs, music, comedy, hobbies, and social activities would improve communication skills to build up confidence, trust, professional attitudes, and happy relationships.

Behavior and Personality

Personality is the perceivable part of human behavior. It is the interface between human genes and the environment. Genetic factors determine the thresholds of human instinctive behaviors or the inherited personality traits, while environment conditions or pollutes the human genetic behavior according to cultural traditions, values, and beliefs. For example, children born with high ego thresholds tend to be abusive, but environment can shrink or expand their inherited ego thresholds and generate an acquired ego belief system. Such environmental transformations make people in India behave differently from those in China or Europe.

Family is the seed for personality, and the culture is the soil in which the seeds grow. After birth, children acquire a certain language, body language, accent, and lifestyle depending on their family's social class, belief, behavior, education, and cultural norms. Culture manufactures different human models at each time and place, and in each culture, the human personality is judged by the person's own role model. People lose many aspects of their inherited personality traits and are programmed differently in each family or culture.

Personality has been classified into types and subtypes, such as extrovert, introvert, thinker, planner, leader, follower, impulsive, peaceful, sociable, fanatic, eccentric, odd, or different. Ironically some people become celebrity, famous or rich, if they change their behavior, dress code, or sexuality. Personality also was ordered as type A, B, C., etc. However, the genetic thresholds of human ego its programming during childhood have major impact on crafting human personality and making siblings' and people's personalities different.

Humans' behavior is linked to their ego belief system and feeling. The majority of humans are living in cultures and are followers of their cultural norms. Only a few people are able to live freely without any cultural influence. People are conditioned to follow law, religious and cultural norms, routines, habits, rituals, or values. They feel uncomfortable, bad, guilty, stressed, worried, or vulnerable to criticisms, shame, bullying or abuse, if they behave against their programmed belief or against their cultural norms. Their negative feelings can affect their daily behaviors, relationships, and productivity.

The human ego is culturally inhibited by fear of the law, taboos, or shame, and most people hide their programmed egos at home and wear masks at work. They may behave in a professional way at work, while at home, they express their egos' desires and enemies. Many marriages don't last long anymore, as people's ego greed has expanded and their real ego personalities are only revealed after marriage. The human ego drives people to fake emotions, feelings, identities, and behaviors in order to gain certain desires. In interviews or on blind dates, people may show care, empathy, and humanity, but at home, they may behave in the opposite way or practice certain habits, rituals, or behaviors that they would otherwise never talk about.

During strong emotions, however, people many react without masks. Provoking people in an interview can help to reveal part of their real personality. This is because strong emotions can bring up the dormant emotional files they saved in their memories during childhood. During crises, people relate to their past saved experiences, which are already programmed into their TEBE pacemaker and the ANS to trigger their negative emotions subconsciously. People may show different reactions every day, but crises can reveal part of their real programmed personalities.

The flare-up of their negative emotions may drive them to lose their temper even in a job interview.

Regardless, people's inherited personality traits, human culture are the basis for people's personalities. Certain cultures remain corrupt or poor for many centuries. Their fanatic cultural beliefs become part of their ego belief system, blinding their insight, preventing them from seeing or accepting the truth or their own mistakes or accepting other behavior or culture. Their belief system cannot be easily changed after childhood, as this can make them feel unconformable, guilty, vulnerable to criticism, rejected, or abused by their culture.

Changing beliefs may be an impossible task in people with high ego thresholds and fixed belief systems, particularly if they keep receiving the same thoughts or media and living in the same environment or subjected to racism by other cultures or media. Members of the common people or royal families feel difficulty in exchanging their cultures after childhood, as they can't acquire new accents, body language, emotional reactions, habits, or behaviors of different social classes.

Sexual Behavior and Sexuality

Sexual desire is an irresistible, instinctive, and impulsive behavior in animals, driving them to copulate to survive and avoid extinction. In humans, sex is not only an instinct but an ego desire to sexually abuse, rape, humiliate, or stigmatize a person or for bonding to a person with certain physical looks or of a certain age, gender, bank credit, assets, race, religion, or nationality to achieve ego pleasure, meet personal or emotional needs, or to satisfy ego greed.

Sex in humans is an addictive ego heroin and a magnetic power that drives strangers to make physical contact or visit sex venues. The pleasure of stimulating sexual organs is associated with erotic and irresistible ego-favorite emotions or energy, such as lust, passion, fantasy, attention, tension, obsession, compulsion, submission, domination, foreplay, play, preorgasm, orgasm, and relaxation. Orgasm is followed by ejaculation and a recovery period in men, while women can have multiple orgasms or none during sex.

Unlike men, women are more emotional sexual beings. They can give and receive love without sex, while men can give and receive sex without love. Women can sleep in the same bed without having sex, while men tend to have an involuntary morning erection, which can stimulate them to have sex with their sleeping partner. Men are more "sexual animals" than women. The joy of sex can make men obsessed with sex, promiscuous, submissive, distrustful, or unfaithful. Sex in men has driven them to watch, flirt, seduce, harass, chase, pay, or fight for a woman since the beginning of time or to masturbate, watch porn, or engage in polygamy, orgy, paraphilia, rape, and wasting time and money to travel abroad for legal or illegal sex.

The pleasure of pre-ejaculation and orgasm in men is narcotic, hypnotic, sedating, and addictive. It can delete their willpower to resist ejaculation and make them preconscious, impulsive animals, may commit rape without considering others. Sex in men is an ego personal need and/or greed. Even after marriage, men may keep staring at women's faces, physical looks, or body parts (breasts, buttocks) in public places or at work. In women, sex is an ego emotional need and/or satisfaction. They are more emotionally attached and faithful to their ego-desirable person or to their children than men. They have instinctive and/or cultural pressures to have children within their fertility period, which starts at puberty and usually ends at menopause. Men's fertility period also starts at puberty and may last until death.

Human sexuality includes all mental and physical conscious, subconscious, and unconscious sexual thoughts, feelings, desires, reactions, behaviors, fantasy and dreams. It is influenced by genes and the mother's medical and hormonal status during pregnancy, as well as culture, religion, taboos, law, media, personal belief systems, and early emotional and sexual experience. Acquired factors play a major part in human sexuality.

Sexual feeling is related to the human ego belief system, while sexual behavior is related to cultural and ego inhibitions. Without ego inhibition, (e.g., law, punishment, religion, taboo, shame or stigma) men may practice any sexual behavior. However, the level of the ego's inhibition can make certain people promiscuous or stay virgins for life, even without masturbation.

Animals may masturbate or have sex in the wild, but in humans, masturbation and sex are unacceptable in public places; hence, it is difficult to measure the prevalence of masturbation and each type of sexual behavior in both sexes, in every culture, and in every century. Additionally, it may be impossible to measure sexual thoughts and feelings generated by both men and women on a daily basis; therefore, the prevalence of each type of sexual orientation may never be accurately estimated.

Masturbation can be difficult to achieve without hands or without frequent touch stimulation of sex organs while fantasizing about an ego desirable person or watching porn. Digital social media, dating agents, and the sex industry have flourished over the last few decades, and more satellite channels and websites have become available, presenting different kinds of sexual behaviors and promoting the use of different types of fetishes and sex toy products. Behavior is stimulating, and the media stimulates the curious ego to try different types of sexual pleasure, including abusive sex. Frequent masturbation every day may affect sleep rhythms, concentration, and work performance, and this habit may continue after marriage, affecting libido, sexual performance, or sexual relationships.

As I said in my previous book, ejaculation in men requires frequent touch stimulation of the "ejaculation spot," or "E-spot." This spot is located in the clitoris in women and under the glans (head) of the penis in men. It becomes swollen and firm before ejaculation. In men, ejaculation can't be achieved easily after amputation of this spot or the distal part of the penis. Without the E-spot, it would be difficult to have human generation or reproduction.

Premature ejaculation in men can be prevented by avoiding touching this spot before the feeling of orgasm. The stimulation of the E-spot can create submissive and irresistible erotic feelings in men, which can be prolonged for hours by careful, gentle on and off touch stimulation of this spot. The anal spot, or A-spot, is another sensitive zone that can induce sexual submission, but it is not directly related to ejaculation.

Sexuality is influenced by feeling, and human feeling is influenced by thoughts, ego belief system, and behaviors.

Behavior is stimulating, and romantic movies or porn stimulate children's ego curiosity and appetite for sex, just like junk food stimulates their appetite to eat. Seeing delicious food causes secretion of saliva in the mouth, and watching a desirable sexual object triggers the ANS to dilate sex organs with blood, causing sex organ arousal and genital secretion, or "pre-ejaculate" in men and vaginal discharge in women. However, unlike eating, sexual behavior is unacceptable in public; hence, most human sexual behavior remains secretive in many cultures.

Sexual feeling is acquired by learning experiences during childhood through exposure to sexual chats, stories, images, movies, thoughts, actions, or experiences. In the city, children's TEBE is programmed by family, culture, fairy tales, books, or media to be judgmental in recognizing the ego-desirable person (e.g., young, beautiful, tall, slim, rich, powerful, or brave) and ego-undesirable person (e.g., old, ugly, short, fat, poor, weak, or soft). This programming evolves from an ego judgment "belief" into fantasy and personal expectations of ego desirable and undesirable persons. Gradually, the programmed ego belief system conditions the ANS to generate "acquired feelings" (e.g., good, bad, repulsive, or erotic feelings), when meeting a desirable or ugly person.

Children are stimulated by reading about idols or heroes, by actions, or by romantic movies. Boys may copy their idols and compete with their peers to attract the attention of a beautiful girl or build dreams to marry an ego-desirable girl. Before puberty, their love is free from sex, as penile erection starts at puberty.

At puberty, sex organs start to enlarge and become sensitive to touch. Boys develop involuntary erections, have morning erections, and may experience nocturnal emissions (wet dreams). Nudity becomes taboo. Nude men may not be able to control their erections in public, and some people or cultures develop curiosity about or obsession with the size of the penis (more so than the size of the universe).

Without parents' care and discipline or role models, children's fantasies and emotions can grow in different directions or along spectra. In the jungle, children follow their tribe's limited traditions. In the cities, children may learn a wide range of sexual behaviors. Although they are programmed to marry from the same age group, social class, education level, race, or religion, their sexual activity is influenced by their programmed ego desire and emotional status and by the sexual thoughts and experiences they come across in their environments.

In conservative cultures, men and women are programmed to play certain roles. Women are under pressure of cultural traditions to marry and have children. This can force some women to marry an ego-undesirable person or a person with unknown sexual history. Their sexual behavior can be influenced by their husbands' personal, emotional, medical, psychological, and financial status. Men are freer than women to express their sexuality and choose their ego-desirable person. In many cultures, women and children are still financially dependent on men and can be subjected to all types of abuses—emotional, financial, physical, and sexual.

With more financial independence, equality, civil rights, and contraception in developed countries, women become freer to express their sexuality and are able to divorce their husbands and have independent personal and sexual lives. However, the ego greed for money, financial security, pleasure, or sex can drive men and women to seek divorce or legal aid to gain part of their partner's fortune, income, or social benefits, without considering their children's needs, feelings, or well-being. In contrast, staying with an abusive parent may also affect children's well-being.

No gay, straight, incest, rape, or pedophilia gene has been discovered yet. Human sexuality starts as an acquired sensory stimulation and evolves into thoughts, ego beliefs, feelings, and behaviors. Sexual orientation is a feeling, with or without behavior, while sexual behavior is a physical activity with or without feeling. Humans' feelings are related to their acquired beliefs, thoughts, and behaviors. If sexuality is only genetic, we would expect a fixed prevalence rate of each sexual behavior. However, genes do not determine the type of our family, culture, or media. Porn market is flourishing and the human ego is curious to try different types of sexual pleasure, more than before. A couple or group of men or women may lose their inhibitions through the abuse of alcohol or drugs and may practice different levels of bisexual or homosexual activities while watching porn.

Genes can determine our inherited ego and emotional thresholds and personality traits but do not determine our family or culture or the daily TV or media programs, sexual events, sexual abuses, and porn in our environment. Genetic thresholds make siblings or twins express different thoughts, interests, perceptions, and degrees of emotion, but environment (family, culture, and media) can expand or shrink human ego behavior and generate acquired ego expectations and feeling. The human ego can't live without pleasure or abuse. A caveperson would acquire similar sexual thoughts, fantasies, expectations, feelings, and behavior as modern people if exposed to the same temptations, romantic movies, or porn.

Sex is not essential for human health but important for reproduction and ego greed. A caveman would have no sexual feeling if he was born alone on an island. His ego curiosity for sex would begin when he learned, saw, heard, or watched sex. He might watch sex between animals and try it, or he might wait for the first person to arrive on the island. If he was living only with men, he might have homosexual sex. If he was living only with women, he might have heterosexual sex. If both sexes arrived on the island, he would follow cultural norms or marriage. However, his sexuality would not evolve in different directions without him hearing, feeling, or watching different types of sexual behaviors available in his environment.

Just like infants, a caveman wouldn't describe, fantasize, or feel things he had never seen, felt, touched, tasted, or heard before. In the Stone Age, there were no lipsticks, makeup, short skirts, high heels, junk food, perfumes, supermarkets, flower shops, money, smartphones, or sports cars. They became a source of ego need, greed, and expectations that induced comfort or happy feelings. After having the above temptations, the insecure ego may feel bored and keep searching for more.

Children are exposed to different daily behaviors, which program their curious egos to be judgmental, expressing different desires, enemies, wishes, and expectations of good and bad values within their culture. Their programmed ego judgment, or belief, determines their perceptions, expectations, and future feelings. In return, their feelings can influence their beliefs and behaviors. Sexual feeling may be inhibited by cultural taboos, traditions, or law, but children and adults may practice their fantasies or certain sexual behaviors secretly when their ego greed undermines their beliefs.

Sexual behavior is not always influenced by sexual feelings, or beliefs, but the level of ego inhibition or willpower. A man with a high ego threshold (arrogant, abusive, dominant, greedy, careless, or ruthless) tends to emotionally, physically, or sexually abuse a weaker person in any culture. Even if he is physically weak, he might make allies or a gang to express his evil ego energy. Children, adolescents, or adults with high genetic or acquired ego thresholds in schools, neighborhoods, work, the military, or in prisons may sexually abuse a weaker person, and not all of them "feel" homosexual. Their arrogant ego drives them to shame and stigmatize their victims with homosexuality.

In the city, children are exposed to massive external sensory stimuli and develop a long list of ego-desirable and ego-enemy persons or objects, which programs their TEBE pacemaker to react with a spectrum of feelings, ranging from happy to abusive. Their conditioned ego reacts, judges, and generates different acquired expectations, values, and perceptions. Their feelings follow their ego belief or expectations of desirable persons (tall, strong, fair skin, slim, muscular, or wearing certain uniforms, or fashions). At home, in the neighborhood, or at school, the egos of boys and girls compare and compete with each other in their physical looks, personal processions, sports, or school performances. They may feel good or bad about themselves, and their feelings influence their confidence, communication, interaction, performance, and their conscious and subconscious sexual behavior.

During adolescence, children's hormonal peaks make them moody, sensitive, mentally and emotionally unstable, and vulnerable to abusive behaviors. Their insecure egos can make them rebels when they receive negative comments or rejection or experience failure or abuse. Their ego curiosity may drive them to copy the behavior of adults in their environment or in the media (e.g., lifestyles of celebrities, politicians, or religious leaders or the practice of cultural rituals and sports or the watching of games, TV, or movies). Their programmed ego judges the people in movies differently and generates different expectations, thoughts, and fantasies. Their early romantic thoughts, emotions, and behavior stimulate the ANS (before or after puberty) and fix sexual events in the memory with sexual thoughts and emotions for years or for good and influence their sexual orientation.

In conservative culture, taboos, shame, or stigma against sex prevents children and adults from expressing their sexual orientation or feelings. Their growing sexual feelings may become powerful subconscious ego energy and can make them shy or shaky in front of an ego-desirable person they meet. Without inhibition, the ego is curious to copy any pleasurable behavior, including painful sexual behavior, such as inserting painful objects in the vagina or anus. Such behaviors were used to torture prisoners, but the narcotic power of sex can make humans the most submissive animal.

Sex gives great ego pleasure but for a short time and is not free of conflict. It can lead to sexual abuse, incest, rape, emotional unrest, and STDs/HIV. Most religions and cultures restricted men's sexual freedom to heterosexual marriage, and heterosexuality became a norm. Nonetheless, despite the law and taboos, homosexuality, transgender identity, incest, rape, pedophilia, and paraphilia have continued as secretive behaviors throughout human history. Conservative cultures may accept corruption, cheating, adultery, infidelity, and human rights abuses but reject males behaving in a feminine way. Such men can be subjected to insults, shame, abuse, or rape, as can the male who receives anal sex from another male. In contrast, a man who shares anal sex with another man tends to be proud of his sexual act.

Sexual orientation starts before puberty. Children are born biemotional. They have emotions for both parents and genders, but their inherited emotional thresholds vary and their parents may not share equal emotions or competent to manage their emotions or their children emotions and needs. Without support or discipline, the curious children's ego searches for pleasure in the surrounding environment, e.g., the media, TV, books, journals, and games. Their ego starts to perceive their surroundings and develop different expectations and values. They compare themselves and their families with what they see in the media or with their peers' families in wealth, possessions, houses, cars, happiness, hobbies, interests, holidays, gifts, or toys. They develop different perceptions or feelings about themselves and others.

A boring, useless, absent father can drive the son to be attached to his mother or "soft" peers. He may learn to copy women's behaviors, conversations, or lifestyles. The boy may feel more comfortable playing with girls than with his boring or abusive father or siblings.

Gradually, the boy may copy or express feminine behavior. Some boys are brought up by strict religious parents who perceive sex with women as a sin may feel all women are like their mother or sister (not for sex). Boys who live with negative women (e.g., complaining, and crying all the time, superficial, or dismissive) may subconsciously programmed to avoid having relationships with women. Some boys may feel unattractive and after frequent rejections by girls, lose confidence in making relationships with girls or they may feel more comfortable being with boys.

At puberty, children start to compare their bodies with their peers' or celebrities' and according to their culturally programmed ego. They develop different perceptions, expectations, and feelings toward themselves and toward others. Without supportive parents, their culturally programmed ego subconsciously judges people as ego desirable or undesirable. A short, skinny, or fat boy may perceive himself as unattractive, weak, or inferior and lose confidence in front of a tall, strong, or confident boy. He may feel sexually attracted to him, but his feeling does not necessarily evolve into a sexual act. Early childhood sexual feelings may change into a subconscious fantasy and drive him to masturbate to fulfill his sexual urges.

Such early experience can program the ANS to release H/N and "glue" the sexual thoughts in the memory, programming the TEBE pacemaker and ANS to subconsciously react (become sexually aroused) when seeing, thinking, talking to or about, watching, or meeting an ego-desirable person. The TEBE pacemaker may keep generating homosexual wet dreams for good, which may make him "feel" bad, abnormal, guilty, or unable to have an erection or sex with women. The feeling can't be easily deleted, as it is linked to the powerful ego belief that females can't make him sexually aroused and only certain ego-desirable males can. In conservative culture, he may attempt or commit suicide or may marry but keep using his saved or dormant homosexual thoughts or fantasies to reach orgasm during sex or masturbation.

Emotional depravation or emotional hunger among children brought up by broken, dysfunctional families is another factor for making children vulnerable to paraphilia or to being victims of sexual abuse or abusers. Emotionally, physically, or financially abused boys develop an emotional hanger to be loved or supported. Without family support, they may lose confidence, feel unfairness, or feel trapped in an abusive family they can't rid of. They may search for support and may feel inferior or submissive to a confident or physically attractive, stronger, or richer peer or may become loners, rebels, or antisocial or show dominant abusive behavior to attract attention. In contrast, children in supportive families gain love and confidence, enabling them to resist ego temptation.

The human ego can't live without curiosity, greed, pride, vanity, judgment, pleasure, abuse, or counterabuse. It gets bored easily. Lack of a father and/or mother role in the family can drive children's egos to search for support, love, or pleasure. Playing is an instinct in all animals, and children's egos get bored from having the same play or toys. Bored children may look for more pleasurable behavior, such as eating, watching TV, playing video games, smoking, shopping, or watching movies. Some children may develop addictions to food, games, the Internet, or masturbation. Their addictive behavior can make them short-tempered, moody, impulsive, abusive, or vulnerable to abuse or to mental illnesses.

Children's psychology is different from an animal's psychology. Many parents have a strong ego desire to have children, but they are incompetent to look after a pet. Children need personal, medical, psychological, financial, and educational care and support for eighteen years or until they become independent. It is no surprise that human history repeats itself in abuse and prisons continue to host criminals, including sex offenders. Parents are the first abusers if they are irresponsible or incompetent to look after their children until they become independent.

Parents have the choice to have sex and make children, but children have no choice but to accept their parents' mental and financial status. They may dislike, distrust, or hate their parents and choose an ego-desirable peer, friend, relative, neighbor, or stranger who gives them comfort, pleasure, attention, gifts, or joy or fulfills their emotional hunger and curiosity. At the same time, they may become vulnerable to emotional, physical, financial, and sexual abuse.

Child abuse is common in male-biased cultures, where it is acceptable for men to be irresponsible and abusive and to have many children left to be fed by "God." Sadly, millions of poor children suffer poverty and health problems or acquire HIV infection from their infected mothers during pregnancy, mainly because their selfish, infected fathers hide their affairs before or after marriage.

Disorder of gender identity is another spectrum of urban ego behavior, and it is probably rare in the jungle. In the Stone Age, there were no high heels, nail polish, or hair spray, and people did not sell their bodies for money. A beautiful smooth and soft female can attract the attention of any male regardless their sexual orientation. Although modern society has produced many beauty products and "sexy" women, femininity is on the decline. In many cultures femininity is undermined by the ego greed to compete with men. This can deter men from powerful women. In contrast, smooth, beautiful, feminine women in the media or celebrities can become fantasy for many men. They may marry but they keep their fantasy to certain celebrities.

Behavior is stimulating and reflective. A supportive relationship between a father and the male infant can give boys the sense of male belonging and gender identity. The same can occur between a female child and her supportive mother. During early childhood, spoiled or neglected children may become closer to their comfortable mother or celebrity fans than their useless or absent father. They may develop feminine interests, fantasies and curiosity to copy glamorous actresses' behaviors, or fashion to fulfill their ego or emotional hunger or to alleviate boredom. Without inhibition, their curious egos may copy any sexual behavior to make them "feel good," including cross-dressing or practicing other-gender habits and behaviors. Their TEBE becomes gradually programmed to feel good practicing such behaviors.

During adulthood, they may continue to secretly practice cross-dressing to give them pleasure or to escape their boring reality. Some adolescents and adults may attempt suicide, especially after a homosexual experience, as they cannot stop their subconscious homosexual thoughts and feelings or sexual arousal toward a person of the same sex. However, homosexuality has started to become acceptable behavior in many Western countries. This may decrease the rate of suicide but can increase the rate of STDs among people practicing unsafe sex.

Sex is a wonderful, mutual human behavior with a trustworthy person, but most sexual relationships are based on ego desire, which usually lacks trust; even within a marriage, spouses may cheat on each other. Without superego, marriages may end quickly; the children will suffer from behavior and personal relationship difficulties. In the cities, not all children have supportive or responsible parents, and they may end up with different sexual thoughts, feelings, and behaviors or end up in the hands of a pedophilic peer, relative, or stranger.

Sex addiction and prostitution are products of a selfish civilization. Sexually addicted people may become submissive, giving their bodies to please others. In brothels, men or women may lose their willpower and bodies for a sexually desirable person. In contrast, a sexually desirable or physically attractive person may only choose attractive younger people, leaving the unattractive, old, or weak person to suffer shame or rejection. Additionally, the risk of STDs (like HIV) is higher in casual, unprotected sex compared with monogamous sex. Even unprotected oral sex can cause the transmission of many STDs, including herpes, gonorrhea, syphilis, and HIV.

Luckily, animals do not have sanity to expand their ego greed, emotions, thoughts, feelings, and sexual behavior. They do not develop sex addictions or have the desire to kill for money. Animals' sexual behavior remains an inherited, unconditioned impulse. They have no sexual fantasies to commit extreme sexual behavior, and they are unable to have sex for money or several days with multiple partners and in different positions with or without emotions (see diagram 3).

	Animal Sexual Response	Human Sexual Response
1	Inherited (unconditioned)	Learned (conditioned)
2	No related to sanity	Related to sanity elements
3	Not related to physical looks	Related to physical attraction or looks
4	Not liable to obsession	Liable to fantasy, obsession, addiction
5	Instinctive impulse (irresistible)	May stay virgin or promiscuous for decades
6	Starts after puberty	Sexual abuse start before puberty
7	Limited behaviour	Can be extreme
8	Lasts for a few minutes	Can last for hours or days
9	Ends by orgasm or ejaculation	Ends by leaving the sexual fantasy/object
10	Not influenced by culture	Influenced by culture, media, drugs, mental problems

Diagram -3: Shows the difference between animal and human's sexual response.

SUMMARY

Thinking is generated by a TEBE, or mind pacemaker, which represents the subconscious mind and is dominated by ego desires. The TEBE produces continuous thoughts or "mind beats" during the day and dreams during sleep.

Human "mind beats" subconsciously relate to childhood programming. Children save life events as emotional thoughts in the memory for many decades. These thoughts influence their feelings, behavior, beliefs, and sexuality.

The ego is a progressive and destructive human energy that drives people to have selfish desires, goals, or dreams without considering others. The ego can't live without curiosity, pride, vanity, judgment, pleasure break, greed, and abuse. Its threats charge humans with obsessive hate and anger toward its enemies.

The human ego's curiosity expands through motivation, inspiration and temptations. It has made people creative and inventive, but its pride, greed, and addiction to pleasure or abuse make humans insecure, and distrustful. It drove the cavepeople to reach the moon but kept them obsessed with their ego desires and threats.

People make ego enemies more than ego desires. Any threat to their ego desires becomes an enemy, triggering stress, fear, hate, and anger. These negative emotions form an energy that is harmful to human immunity and humanity. It can cause insomnia, depression, and psychosomatic and mental-health illnesses and wars.

Genes manufacture physical looks, emotions, and ego thresholds, while culture manufactures people with certain specifications: language, accent, body language, traditions, reactions, rituals, values, beliefs, feelings, and mentality.

It might be is easier to understand life as an illusion rather than as real. Living without a culture shrinks the human ego. Living within a culture "pollutes" authentic, inherited instincts with acquired, programmed "cultural software."

Many religions are based on the "ego desire" to end up in heaven and send the ego enemy to hell. This has programmed multiple generations with subconscious rejection toward people from other faiths or toward atheists. It was one of the main sources of human conflict, abuse, and wars against the ego enemy.

Sex is an "ego heroin." It is addictive behavior that generates a high dose of temporary ego-favored emotions. The first child abusers are the selfish or irresponsible parents, who are incapable of looking after children's emotional, educational, and financial needs and protecting them.

The human mind can't think without relating to the past, and many people live in the past. History books are based on ego pride and ego enemy. Human history is repeating itself, as the human ego can't live without pride, greed, pleasure, or abuse.

Changing cultures requires inspiring "egoless" leadership. Changing people's mentality requires changing their ego belief system, changing their environment, and deprogramming the TEBE pacemaker to generate new feelings and behaviors.

Happiness starts from within by changing thoughts and behavior. Our abusive past is irrelevant to the future we wish to make. Positive thinking and nonjudgmental professional behavior make the way for progress. Anger blinds the mind to the truth, our mistakes, and the rights of our ego enemies.

Accepting the worst, or death, can kill the ego. Skipping the ego, history books, childhood abuse, drama, violence, and racist, political, and religious bias can stop anger and the mind from making ego enemies and may cure many mental illnesses.

Although humans are "polluted" with cultural norms, unlike other mammals, they can fantasize and fly from the past to the future. They can change their beliefs and feelings by starting to recognize that their bodies and souls interface with the environment—air, sea, birds, animals, plants, planets, galaxies, and the universe.

We may never forgive our ego enemies, but we can shrink our anger by practicing nonjudgmental, positive behavior, which enables us to make followers instead of enemies. The "power of behavior" is the marker of belief. A bad behavior is a bad religion and vice versa. Every day, we play a role in life's theater. Nonjudgmental, positive, ethical, and professional behavior can make ego enemies into fans.

I hope racist religious people earn their titles in humanity to inspire their ego enemies. I dream of when political leaders can provide regular assessments in each town to uncover all types of child abuse (physical, emotional, financial, and sexual) within or outside children's homes, so these children can be offered support, protection, or rescue.

Humans have been abusing and killing other humans and animals for millions of years. It would cause no harm to make international superego days, e.g., donation day, forgiving day, hand-shaking and smiling day, zero-abuse day, elderly support day, children-support day, patient-visiting day, animal-support day, vegetarian day, green day, laughing day, and singing or dancing day to prove that the "human herd" can be more caring and peaceful than the animal herds.

Glossary

ANS. Autonomic nervous system. Part of the human nervous system, consisting of sympathetic and parasympathetic systems that work involuntarily and secrete chemicals and hormones to control human body physiology during emotions.

CNS. Central nervous system.

ego enemy. Anything rejected by the ego (e.g., person, place, culture, faith)

ego injury. Pride, injury, or shame resulting from failure to achieve self-desires.

ego threat. Anything that prevents or interferes with achieving self-desire.

ego. Human selfish energy to have or act without considering others.

E-spot. Located in the clitoris in women and under the glans penis in men.

H/Ns. Hormones and neurotransmitters released with emotions.

IBS. Irritable bowel syndrome.

mind beats. Subconscious thought beats generated by the mind pacemaker.

OCD. Obsessive compulsive disorder.

sanity elements. New concept in simplifying human sanity into ten elements.

self-conditioning. Programming of the human mind with cultural behavior and habits.

STD. Sexually transmitted disease.

TEBE pacemaker. Acronym meaning *thinking, ego, belief,* and *emotions.* This is a mind pacemaker and is the source of human thinking.